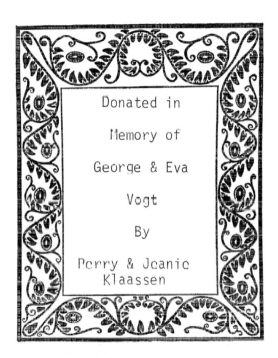

Donated in

Memory of

George & Eva

Vogt

By

Perry & Jeanie
Klaassen

ORIGINS OF
CONCEPTS IN
HUMAN BEHAVIOR
social and cultural factors

MARK D. ALTSCHULE

The Francis A. Countway Library of Medicine
Harvard Medical School

HEMISPHERE PUBLISHING CORPORATION

Washington   London

A HALSTED PRESS BOOK

JOHN WILEY & SONS

New York   London   Sydney   Toronto

PHOTO CREDITS

Page 5: courtesy of Alinari/Scala. Reprinted by permission.

Page 19: from Laverdierre, C.-H. *Oeuvres de Champlain, publees sous le patronage de l'Universite Laval.* 2nd ed. Quebec: G.-E. Desbarats, 1870.

Page 75: courtesy of the Museo del Prado. Reprinted by permission.

Page 165, top: "The Cure for Lunacy," courtesy of the Museo del Prado. Reprinted by permission.

Page 165, bottom: "The Cure for Folly," courtesy of the Rijksmuseum Amsterdam. Copyright Fotocommissie Rijksmuseum Amsterdam. Reprinted by permission.

Page 167: from the Ars Medica Collection of the Philadelphia Museum of Art. Courtesy of the Pennsylvania Academy of the Fine Arts. Reprinted by permission

Pages 22, 35, 51, 65, 67, 85, 98, 123, 126, 129, 133, 135, 137, 140, 142, 153, 156, 170, 183, and 193: courtesy of the Rare Books Collection, Francis A. Countway Library of Medicine, Harvard Medical School. Reprinted by permission.

Hemisphere Publishing Corporation
1025 Vermont Ave., N.W., Washington, D.C. 20005

Distributed solely by Halsted Press, a Division of John Wiley & Sons, Inc., New York.

1 2 3 4 5 6 7 8 9 0 D O D O 7 8 3 2 1 0 9 8 7

Library of Congress Cataloging in Publication Data

Altschule, Mark David.
   Origins of concepts in human behavior.

   Includes index.
   1. Psychiatry—History—Addresses, essays, lectures.
2. Medicine—History—Addresses, essays, lectures.
3. Humanism—Addresses, essays, lectures. I. Title.
RC338.A47   616.8'9   76-46320
ISBN 0-470-99001-5

Printed in the United States of America

CONTENTS

INTRODUCTION

The human mind is made uneasy by unembellished ideas presented simply and precisely. It prefers analogy and metaphor. These have produced much poetry but are used mostly because they have the advantage of meaning anything that anybody wants them to mean. History is widely—though not universally—regarded as a form of literature, and hence is related to poetry. Those who believe that it is a form of literature must believe that metaphor and analogy play a prominent place in all historical writing. It is no surprise, therefore, that History, or rather its progenitor, Time, is often described as a river. This conceit, although pretty, is more likely to confuse than to clarify. For example, Francis Bacon said in 1620, "Time, like a river, bears down to us that which is light and inflated, and sinks that which is heavy and solid." This is clear enough, but Baron Ernst von Feuchtersleben, dean of the Medical School at Vienna and councilor to Emperor Francis Joseph, expressed it differently. In 1845 he wrote, "Newly discovered books, like newly discovered ores, may be rich or poor; but to test their value, they require that the stream of time should flow over them, which fails not to carry away what is light and worthless, and leave the sterling metal behind."

In discussing newly rediscovered ancient ideas, we are forced to conclude that von Feuchtersleben's idea is not valid, because it implies that Time, if left alone, will reveal what is best. Bacon's idea describes my aim and procedure in writing this

1

book: I have attempted to dredge up what the river Time has submerged.

Those who have seen what seems to be a steady stream of redundant learned volumes may want to know what motivated the present work. For one thing, it might be viewed as a stimulus to thought. Most learned works are presented as an orderly sequence of definitive items and as such are likely to stultify thinking. The learned have a propensity for ceasing to think when they encounter a well-organized scholarly work. Such works are eminently useful to beginners, but they are likely to present a false view of steadily, inevitably advancing knowledge that does not accord with the history of learning. Only those who recognize the gaps and inconsistencies in such works will find them a stimulus to thought. The present work aims to show that basic ideas—at least in psychiatry—do not develop according to an orderly, inevitable scheme.

There is another idea that stimulated the writing of this book. This idea relates to the need for certain elements in the nature of medicine to be pointed out. The nature of medicine has been the subject of discussion by many, with diverse results. On the one hand, it is clear that medicine can never be a science, although it borrows methods and concepts from the sciences. Similarly medicine can never be an art; although physicians must often be artful, they are rarely required to be artistic. From the operational viewpoint medicine is simply a profession, with specific aims, approaches, methods, and thought patterns, all of which are unique to it, either as such or else in the manner of their application. From the philosophic viewpoint medicine must be considered a humanity.

A humanist is, by definition, one whose way of life emphasizes human interests and is based specifically on a concern for restoring, maintaining, or enhancing the dignity of individuals and their value to themselves and their community. According to this characterization, all good physicians are humanists. Few of them, however, are humanitarians, that is, persons devoted to the idea that collective human welfare requires organized social (rather than political) reform. The humanism of good physicians is so completely taken for granted that it is often ignored. This is unfortunate, for clinical medicine would benefit if its humanism were brought strongly to the attention of both laymen and physicians. This has been done only occasionally. Different methods have been used to call attention to humanistic aspects of clinical medicine. Most of these infrequent discussions are in a philosophic vein, which although spiritually elevating are likely to be too vague to be informative and in any case make heavy reading.

In the present work the humanistic nature of medicine has been made evident through its history. The actual approach was justified by a recent comment by Lynn White, Jr. In a technical discussion of a highly specific subject in medieval art history, he casually interposed a profound statement that described the role of the humanist, and by implication defined his aim. White wrote, "The guild of humanists will not have reached maturity until we produce a global history of cultures that is more than a rough mosaic of adjacencies."

Any history such as White envisions is beyond reach today, but individual sectors of it may be so handled to a limited degree. The present work attempts this approach with respect to a few items of medical history. In each case the data presented show that medical history is neither linear nor isolated. It goes back and forth, to one direction and another, joining with and then diverging from other aspects of known history. By taking from and contributing to whatever cultural milieus prevail at the time, medicine shows itself, in a persistent and often fumbling way, to participate in the aims of humanism.

The inextricably interwined relations between medicine and other aspects of society become most evident when both are changing. This has been brought out convincingly in two recent scholarly works, Darnton's *Mesmerism* (1968) and Hill's *The World Turned Upside Down* (1972). It is clear that romantic social revolutions are accompanied—and influenced—by the rise of nutty medical movements. During periods of unsensational social evolution, the accompanying medical changes are likely to be so prosaic as to escape general attention. However, it must not be concluded that all aspects of a change in human thinking that occur during one period or another are equally striking—one change may stand out to such a great extent as to create the impression that it is not related to other contemporary factors.

All these facts justify the creation of the present volume.

The topics discussed here were collected by chance. One topic after another, over a period of twenty years, caught my attention and engaged my interest. Some of the articles were completed in a few months. Others required years to be worked out. Some grew out of talks given at the Countway Library of Medicine, and others may serve for future talks at that institution. The Rare Books Department of the Library has had a special role in the creation of these studies. In many instances it provided the stimulus; in all cases it provided source materials, and on every occasion it served as the locus appropriate to the development of the individual themes. As a uniquely great cultural resource, this department provided the setting for a series of discussions, oral and written, that exemplify what all good medical practitioners know—that clinical medicine develops out of, exists in, and contributes to the cultural milieu, no matter what that milieu happens to be.

REFERENCES

1. Bacon, F. *The advancement and proficiencie of learning* (1620). G. Wats, ed. London: T. Williams., 1674, p. 6.
2. von Feuchtersleben, E. *The principles of medical psychology.* H. E. Lloyd, trans. London: Sydenham Society, 1845, p. IV.
3. Darnton, R. *Mesmerism and the end of the enlightenment in France.* Cambridge, Mass.: Harvard University Press, 1968.
4. Hill, C. *The world turned upside down.* New York: Viking Press, 1972.

Chapter 1

THE PNEUMA CONCEPT
OF THE SOUL

Levitation of St. Francis of Assisi, from a mural (attributed to Giotto) in the upper chapel of the Church of St. Francis at Assisi. The saint is seen rising, apparently propelled by a cloud of vapor, while an airborne observer circles the site. The scene reminds one of recent events at Cape Canaveral, Florida.

The notion that there is a principle called "pneuma" that is responsible for various psychological phenomena was a cornerstone of ancient Greek religion, philosophy, and medicine. Today the concept, if it is considered at all, is usually dismissed as a harmless superstition of an ancient people. Actually the concept was a powerful force in European and Asiatic thinking for several thousand years; in related and modified forms it has affected many different aspects of human thought from the paleolithic age until the present time. Hence it is important for students of the history of psychology to know something about it.

Although the history of the concept antedated the development of Greek philosophy by many centuries, it is best to commence this discussion with the Greek ideas because they are well documented. Intelligent Greeks of the Homeric period believed that consciousness was a manifestation of a vapor called *thymos*, a word probably derived from the Sanskrit *dhumah*; *dhumah* later became the Latin *fumus*. (The word *thymos* survives in the twentieth-century psychiatric term *cyclothymic*.) Some centuries later Greek philosophers apparently came to treat the pneuma concept more systematically. Ancient Greek scientific thought required that there should be one primary substance. Thales, according to Aristotle, chose water as the first principle underlying everything in the universe. Anaximander gave the name Theos, or God, to the undifferentiated substance that filled the universe and became the substance out of which everything in the world was formed. Anaximander was not alone in adhering to this terminology, for Thales also said that all objects were full of gods. Anaximenes believed that the universal substance was air. He said, "As our soul, being air, holds us together, so do breath and air surround the whole universe." Diogenes of Apollonia also negated Thales' ideas about water, stating that air was the life principle.

However, scientific thinking of the time required that the primary substance not only must pervade the entire universe but also must be responsible for all motion. The philosophers therefore believed that since this substance imparted motion to all things that moved, it must be alive; also, since motion was everlasting, the substance must have eternal life. Air seemed to meet all these requirements, specifically the ones involving its relation to life. The philosophers reasoned that we live by breathing, and what we breathe in gives us life; therefore the substance of our souls must be air. The Greek word for soul was *pneuma*, which means breath or air, or *psyche*, which was derived from the word for "to breathe." Similarly the Latin word for soul, *anima*, also meant air and breath. The Greeks thought that the upper air, called *aether*, was so pure as to constitute the highest and most intelligent form of the life principle. Heraklitus said: "We become conscious by inhaling through the breath the Universal Ether, which is Divine Reason." Anaximenes and Anaxagoras believed that the soul was air. Those who believed that everything consisted of atoms modified the belief that the soul was breath or air to fit their own ideas. Democritus, for example, distinguished the soul-particles of air from the rest: "In the air there are many of those particles which are called mind and soul. Hence when we breathe, these enter along with it." This keeps the concentration of mind and soul normal in animals.

The Pythagoreans also believed that "the faculties of the soul are winds," according to Diogenes Laertes. Simplicius quotes Diogenes of Apollonia as saying: "Men and other animals live by means of air, which they breathe in, and this is for them both soul and intelligence. In my opinion that which has intelligence is what is called air by mankind, and by it everything is directed, and it has power over all things; for this in itself seems to me to be God, and to reach everywhere and to arrange everything and to be in everything." Theophrastus asserted that Diogenes said that the Orphics believed that "the air within us is a small portion of the God." Aristotle said that the Orphics believed that "the soul comes in from space as we breathe, borne by the winds." Aristotle believed that the soul was only part air, and that the air only contributed to its function. However, Aristotle's pupils, the Peripatetics, disagreed with this idea and adopted the more ancient view of the soul as pneuma.

In short, many ancient Greek philosophers believed that everything came from air and that air had eternal life, consciousness, and intellect. It gave life to all animals and constituted the thinking part of humans. These beliefs came at a convenient time; in the fifth century B.C. the educated and intelligent had ceased to believe in the anthropomorphic gods of mythology.

The idea that air or breath was divine and constituted the soul or mind of man was not limited to philosophy; it is to be found in other branches of human thought. Thus the poets Aristophanes, Euripides, and Philemon also recognized air as the highest deity among the gods. In the field of religion the Orphics also believed in the creative power of wind. Their account of the creation of the universe stated that the goddess Night was fertilized by the Wind and that their offspring was Eros, who then set the universe in motion. (The idea that Love makes the world go 'round is indeed an ancient one.)

The notion that air was a creative force was accepted in ancient Greek biology. Fertilization of plants, animals, and people by wind is frequently mentioned in Greek myths. The Greeks proved the fertilizing power of air by noting that mares turned their backs to strong winds (ignoring the fact that stallions did also). In the Iliad, Achilles' horses were born to their mother, Podarge, who was impregnated by the wind, Zephyros. In another legend Pandora was made out of clay and then vivified by the Four Winds. Sudden gusts of wind were supposed to enter women's wombs and thereby produce children; babies born without known fathers were called "wind-children."

The idea that the soul was air or breath and that air or breath was the divine creative force was so widespread in ancient Greece that Guthrie (1) properly concluded that the idea must have originated long before the Greeks adopted it. There is evidence that this is so: at one paleolithic burial site a furrow of red earth led to each nostril of the corpse and there was another furrow in front of the mouth; all these arrangements suggested that the people involved in the burial believed that air or breath was at least allied to the soul (2). Other religions expressed or implied a similar belief.

In the ancient Egyptian religion, one god, Khem, represented both the Divine Breath and the Logos. According to the Egyptian belief, the *ka* (the intellectual soul) consisted of breath and shadow. Isis breathed upon the dismembered body of Osiris to restore it to life. The Babylonians believed that the divine word, called *amatu*, pervaded the entire universe and originally set it in motion. Ancient pre-Christian North Slavic peoples believed that the body was inhabited by a soul, called duchu, which left the body in the form of a breath at death. Actually, many primitive peoples believed that the steam that rose from the blood of sacrificial victims represented the departure of the soul.

The Hindus believed that at death "the wind in the body . . . leaves the body, which appears devoid of breath." The equation of breath with soul is also found in the Old Testament—for example, Gen. 2:7, ". . . and breathed into his nostrils the breath of life." The ancient Mayans also equated breath with soul. The Mayan creator-god, Kukulcan, was usually pictured as a feathered serpent or as a man with bird and snake attributes. At times, however, he was represented as ripples on water. This depiction of the effect of breath on water symbolized the act of creating matter. (Some primitive religions held a belief similar to that of Thales that the unformed breath or spirit was the sole creative force. See also Gen. 1:2, "And the Spirit of God moved upon the face of the waters." Likewise John 3:5, "Jesus answered, Verily, verily, I say unto thee, Except a man be born of water and of the spirit, he cannot enter into the kingdom of God.")

The ancient Chinese had beliefs similar to those expressed in the Bible. According to *The Yellow Emperor's Classic of*

Internal Medicine, "The heavenly breath created the earth, the breath of earth created man." Chu Hse, a twelfth-century neo-Confucian, stated that pneuma was the substance of the universe. A tenth-century Jewish writer, Saadiah ben Joseph Fayumi, asserted: "It is in air that the power of the Creator resides and constitutes His existence here below."

Modern primitive peoples still believe that breath is at least part of the soul. This belief exists in Madagascar, Melanesia, and Siberia, and among the Eskimos and the Bantus. Creation of living things by breath or wind is a primitive belief in Australia, New Zealand, the Celebes, and Sumatra, and among Eskimos and North American Indians. The origin of the kiss is of some interest in this respect. Beadnell (3) says that the nose-kiss or sniff-kiss was the most primitive form of that salutation, having arisen in India around 2000 B.C. The word for "kiss" is a variant of "to smell" in the languages of Borneo, Malaya, China, and other lands. The nose-rub of Eskimos and other peoples is clearly related to the sniff-kiss, during which the souls of the kissers mingle or are exchanged.

The idea that breath or wind was soul was not excluded from Christian religious belief. *Pneuma* meant "ghost," that is, the Immortal soul, not only to the ancient Greeks but to St. Luke as well (Luke 24:38). Lactantius, a pre-Nicene father and a contemporary of Origen, likened the entry of the Holy Sprit into Mary to the fertilization of women by wind mentioned recurrently in Greek legends. St. Vincent Ferrer, having turned two coarse fellows into stone, relented and restored them to life by breathing into their mouths. (In another account the pair so treated were illicit lovers whom St. Vincent quickly forgave.) To this day Egyptian Catholic priests (in the Coptic rite) confirm infants, immediately after baptism, by breathing in their faces and saying "receive the Holy Ghost." Similarly, during the ordination of a Coptic bishop, the other bishops present breathe in the new prelate's face (4). These rites were probably suggested by St. John's account of Jesus's first encounter with the disciples after the Resurrection (John 20:22): "He breathed on them, Receive ye the Holy Ghost."

It is evident that divinity and its attributes and extensions, such as the soul, the mind, the state of holiness, were believed to be consequent to the presence of air (the more rarefied, the more divine, as in the form of the aether) and its extensions such as breath and wind. Accordingly, it should be no surprise that saintly persons accumulate rarefied air on aether within them during holy ecstasies or prayer, and thus have lower densities than in ordinary circumstances. The idea that loss of weight is an attribute of holiness is actually pre-Christian. For example, the human heart, which in adults weighs about twelve ounces, was believed to be weighed at death against a feather, by Anubis, the ancient Egyptian deity. Those whose hearts weighed less than the feather were considered to be sufficiently holy to deserve admission to heaven. Many persons of undeniable holiness were reported to have exhibited weightlessness at times, which clearly proves that holiness does cause loss of weight. Thus Sts. Agnes, Albert, Amadeus, Angela of Brescia, Antoinette of Florence, Arey of Gap, Bernard, Catharine of Siena, Peter Celestine (Pope), Clara of Rimini, Coletta, Dominic, Dunstan, Edmund of Canterbury, Francis of Assisi, Francis of Paula, Francis of Posadas, Gerard Mejella, Ignatius Loyola, John of the Cross, Margaret of Hungary, Mary of Egypt, Mary Magdalen de' Pazzi, Monica, Philip Neri, Joseph Oriol, Martin Porres, Stephen of Hungary, Thomas of Florence, Bernadino Realino, Theresa, Francis Xavier, and John of St. Facond as well as a number of Blesseds and Venerables, all were reported to have risen from the ground—sometimes to considerable heights— during prayer or ecstasy. (Father Thurston [5] regards with skepticism the evidence purporting to show levitation in the founders of the Franciscan, Dominican, and Jesuit orders.)

Holy non-Christians were also reported to exhibit weightlessness. One example is Lu Ting-pin, an eighth-century Taoist physician, who was able to fly through the air at will. He won his medical degree at the age of 64, after repeatedly failing his examinations. Nevertheless, owing to a peculiarity of ancient Chinese law, he was able to practice medicine and was worshipped by his patients. Among his hobbies were slaying dragons and overcoming evil.

On the other hand, as Father Thurston (5) has pointed out, from the days of Iamblichus, or even earlier, the number of persons without any claim to sainthood who are said to have been levitated has been considerable. Father Thurston cites one particularly famous case of this sort, whose genuineness was attested to by three witnesses, Lord Lindsay (later the Earl of Crawford), Lord Adare (later the Earl of Dunraven), and Captain Wynne, all of whom affirmed their absolute convictions before a committee of the Dialectical Society and in other circumstances. In the case attested to by these witnesses, a Mr. Home was alleged to have floated out of one window on the third floor at Buckingham Gate and in again through the furthermost window of the next room. The date on which this occurred was December 13, 1868; the three witnesses were all present, but the lights were very low, and one witness said that he saw what happened by the light of the moon. However, the records show that there was a new moon on December 13, 1868. It should be noted that this Mr. Home was the focus of bitter controversies among the Victorian intelligentsia. He was the most noted—or perhaps notorious—medium in the English spiritualist movement. His seances were attended by many prominent persons, including Francis Galton, but he resisted attempts by such scientists as the physicists Tyndall and Faraday, and the physiologic psychologist Carpenter, to investigate his operations. Alfred R. Wallace, the evolutionist who later became Darwin's opponent, tried to convert the skeptics to his own belief, and having failed, he made bitter comments in the lay press, in scientific journals, and even at meetings of the British Association for the Advancement of Science. Wallace was equally unsuccessful with Oliver Wendell Holmes and William James in this country. Wallace's spiritualist faith made it impossible for him to accept Darwin's theory of natural selection (6).

Even in the case of saints who were said to have become weightless, the phenomenon was not always a manifestation of extreme holiness. Thus St. Joseph of Copertino is reported to have flown about above the heads of onlookers uttering "his customary shrill cry," which terrorized the people below. St. Peter of Alcantara also uttered a startling cry when levitated, "creating terror rather than devotion in those present." It was reported that on one occasion when the Blessed Dominic of Jesu Maria rose in the air, a skeptic caught hold of his robe and was carried along, but, becoming frightened, loosed his hold, fell to the ground, and was seriously injured. Moreover, inanimate objects could also be levitated: When St. Philip Neri lost his walking stick in a crowd, he sat down on the steps of the Naples Cathedral and a few minutes later the stick was seen to fly toward him out of the crowd, which cried, "Miracolo! Miracolo!"

In the main, however, the weightless state was far more frequently associated with an increase in holiness than otherwise. There was one interesting exception in the Middle Ages: St. Lidwina, who had so mortified her flesh that she could not move about and had to be wrapped in a sheet to hold her together while being moved, never experienced levitation. Evidently her increased bodily *pneuma* or *aether* leaked out of her too quickly to allow sufficient accumulation to raise her from the ground.

As Father Thurston (5) has noted, the era of levitation of the holy is not over: Sr. Mary of Jesus Crucified (a Carmelite nun of Pau), who died in 1878, was seen to soar through the air to the top of a tree, where one of her slippers was found the next day; Gemma Galganl, who died in 1903, was reported by the local men to have, on occasion, been lifted above the ground in ecstasy; Sr. Maria della Passione, who died in 1912, although infirm in her later years, flew up the stairs, according to a fellow religious, Sr. Maria Prassede of the Adored Crucifix.

The idea that breath is the soul or perhaps some related vital prinicple naturally invaded medicine. Herophilus believed that the arteries were filled with air, the *pneuma zootikon* or *spiritus vitalis*. The persistance for centuries of Herophilus's idea is in accordance with the law of *viability of error*. Hippocrates believed epilepsy to be due to changes in the *pneuma*; he stated, "Consciousness is caused by air."

In the first century A.D. a sect of physicians called Pneumatists was founded in Rome by Atheneus of Attalia; they believed that all disease was due to some abnormal state of the *pneuma*; Atheneus adopted earlier ideas when he said: "The Pneuma is the world soul, the living selfconscious god, from which the souls of men, animals and plants emanate, also the maker and fashioner of all matter." Two centuries later Galen incorporated the pneuma doctrine into his extremely complicated medical dogmas. He apparently believed that pneuma was not the soul itself, but rather the intermediary of the soul in its actions on the body. In this he seems to have been influenced by Aristotle's ideas about the existence of such intermediaries, called entelechies. Galen said that the pneuma was drawn from the outside air into the left ventricle of the heart, where it became "vital spirit." (Some medieval medical texts showed the trachea connecting with the heart.)

Galen's ideas persisted for more than fourteen centuries, either as such or with certain modifications. The great tenth-century compiler, Costa ben Luca, also said that *spiritus* resides in the heart; he added that death occurs when it leaves that organ. According to ben Luca, *spiritus* is swallowed via the mouth. Albertus Magnus also believed that the soul resides in the heart, and that the pulse is due to the motion of *spiritus* in the arteries. However, Alfanus of Salerno, in his work on the pulse, written in the eleventh century, adopted Aristotle's notion of the pneuma as an intermediary between the soul and the body. (Thomas Aquinas also stated that the soul needs an intermediary in order to act on the body.) Paracelsus in the sixteenth century called the force responsible for all activity in the universe the "archeus" and said that in man it resided in the abdomen, from which site it directed and regulated all man's functions. The doctrine that *animal spirits* activated all the body's functions was widely held. Medical writers of the Renaissance and of the seventeenth and eighteenth centuries seem largely to have ignored the relation of their *"animal spirits"* to the *pneuma* or *anima* of the ancients, and indeed for the most part they did not concern themselves with the soul as much as did philosophers and divines. Nevertheless, Thomas Willis, regarded by many as the first modern physician, wrote (in 1683) that the soul "is either a Flame, or a Breath, near to or a-kin to Flame." He based this conclusion on the belief that the soul resides in the blood, which, like flame, needs food and ventilation (7). His debt to Aristotle in this matter is evident. Aristotle in his *Parts of Animals* wrote: "Some maintain that the Soul of an animal is Fire or some such substance. This is a crude way of putting it; and might be improved upon by saying that the Soul subsists in some body of a fiery nature. The reason for this is that the hot substance is the most serviceable of all for the activities of the soul."

Willis's debt to Francis Bacon in this and other respects is also evident. Bacon attempted to distinguish between air and soul and had only succeeded in confusing matters. He started by saying, "The words Air, Sprit, and Soul are sometimes confounded and used for the same thing." He then went on to say that all bodies have a specific spirit and that in addition living bodies have a vital spirit. The first type of spirit, he said "is not a Virtue, an Energy, or a Fiction; but a real, subtile and invisible body, circumscribed by Place and Dimension. Nor again is this spirit Air, any more than the juice of the Grape is water; but a fine attenuated body, a-kin to Air, tho' again, very different from it." A few lines further along in his text he asserted that these spirits "are nearly the same substance with air"; the vital spirits, he declared, resemble "a breath composed of flame and air."

Fragments of ancient ideas about the relations between air and soul turned up in subjects related to medicine. For example, many alchemical texts portrayed the creation of anything at all by means of the symbol for a breath. Other fragments are to be found in early writings in physiology, for example, in writings that interpreted the early experiments that proved the existence of oxygen. John Mayow published the early observations on what he called "nitroaerial spirit" in 1668 and 1674 (8). (We now call this substance oxygen.) He and subsequent commentators listed the attributes of this "spirit": they asserted that it was in the ambient air; that it entered the blood through the lungs; that it vitalized the ovum; that it made the embryo develop; that it was responsible for nutrition, urine formation, and other vital processes; that it produced flame; that it was *vital spirits* (8). In the eighteenth century many physicians replaced "animal spirits" in their thinking with "nervous juice" or even with the "aether" of Newton.

Of course, the concept of *vital spirits* and the related concepts were attacked by eighteenth-century physicians. One of the most outspoken in this regard was Thomas Thompson (9). His criticisms of the advocates of the concept included such statements as: "They differ in the most fundamental Point and first Principle. In order to account mechanically for the Effect of Medicines, the Nature of Diseases, the animal Oeconomy, etc., etc., they have recourse to *animal Spirits*, nervous Juice, or an *Ether infinitely rarified more than ever*. Which are in my humble Opinion manifest Suppositions by no means to be demonstrated, therefore hypothetick Principles. I say if this *Ether*, this nervous Fluid, their animal Spirits, are not demonstrated (they never were yet); a thousand Volumes are turned to waste Paper."

Although the pneuma concept was dropped from most nineteenth-century medical thinking, it persisted in psychology and psychiatry. In the early nineteenth century the English philosopher Jeremy Bentham—now best remembered as the founder of utilitarianism—called psychology *pneumatology*. A school of mental healers called *Pneumatologists* became prominent somewhat later in the nineteenth century. They believed that the soul emitted a "psychical fluid" that "radiating through the body, envelopes the figure in a coloured atmosphere, somewhat resembling steam, only not so palpable." This fluid not only caused the phenomena of mesmerism, they believed, but also made it possible to move objects without touching them. The pneuma concept has now disappeared entirely from medicine except for almost unrecognizable remnants of it in psychoanalytic concepts of the collective unconscious and the superego. In addition, of course, all those who use the word *psyche* or any of its compounds or derivatives to refer to mental phenomena are using a word initially taken from the Greek word for *to breathe*.

It is evident that the pneuma concept of the soul has had a long and complicated history. The concept's apparent origin in the paleolithic era was followed by its association with philosophical and religious ideas about creative breath, a divine word, and a universal intellect. With the passage of time it lost these connections and instead manifested itself in the form of holy weightlessness. It also manifested itself in medical thinking as the concept of so-called vital spirits. With the further passage of time the pneuma concept of the soul ceased to exist as an important part of any system of thought, but it continued to manifest itself in scattered fragments, chiefly in psychiatry. The persistence of remnants of a paleolithic concept of the soul makes the concept one of the most viable of man's many superstitions. Although the concept is no more superstitious than any other current idea about the nature of the mind or soul, it far outranks any of the others in age.

REFERENCES

1. Guthrie, W. K. C. *The Greeks and their gods.* Boston: Beacon Press, 1955.
2. Ackerman, P. The dawn of religions. In *Ancient religions.* V. Ferm, ed. New York: Philosophical Library, 1950.
3. Beadnell, C. M. *The origin of the kiss, and other scientific diversions.* London: Watts, 1942.
4. Attwater, D. *The Christian churches of the East.* Vol. I. *Churches in communion with Rome.* Rev. ed. Milwaukee, Wis · Bunce, 1947.
5. Thurston, H. S. J. *The physical phenomena of mysticism.* Chicago: Henry Regnery, 1952.
6. Kottler, M. J. Alfred Russel Wallace, the origin of man, and spiritualism. *Isis* 65:145, 1974.
7. Willis, T. *The soul of brutes.* London: T. Dring, 1683.
8. Partington, J. R. Some early appraisals of the work of John Mayow. *Isis* 50:211, 1959.
9. Thompson, T. *An historical and critical treatise of the gout: Shewing not only the uncertainty, but danger and presumption of all philosophical systems and hypotheses in physick.* London: H. Hawkins, 1742.

Chapter 2

THE IDEAS OF
THE HURON INDIANS
about the unconscious mind

*Huron Indians. Engravings made from Champlain's drawings, reproduced
from Laverdierre.*

The discovery of various parts of the New World, and the subsequent explorations were to have enormous consequences. The early explorations in Canada are of particular interest as regards certain psychological concepts. These were described in the letters today called *The Jesuit Relations*. The letters are now available in full translation into English (1). This series consisted of full reports from 1632 to 1672; the letters continued after 1672, but in a fragmentary form. These accounts are in many ways more valuable than those of other French explorers because their Jesuit authors lived among the natives more intimately and continuously than any other white men and besides were far better educated than most of the French adventurers and fur traders who entered Canada during that era. The Jesuits studied the natives who lived all along the St. Lawrence River and as far west as the headwaters of the Mississippi, sending back material "gathered from the mouth of the savages." The words quoted here are found in those pages, not once but twice. Father Ragueneau, who preached to the Hurons, had sent back the same report to the Jesuit head-quarters in Paris in two different years, 1648-1649 and 1653.

Besides the free, or at least voluntary desires that we usually have, the Hurons thought that our souls had other desires, in a manner hidden, born in the depth of the soul and projected into some object proportioned to itself. These the philosophers term *desideria innata*, to distinguish them from the desires of which we have knowledge, *desideria elicita*. The soul is thought to reveal its occult desires by means of dreams, which are, as it were, its voice, and if these dreams are fulfilled it remains content; otherwise, it is vexed, and not only no longer seeks good and happiness through the body, but, revolting against this, causes it various infirmities and often death. They therefore diligently observed dreams, in order not to irritate the soul by ignoring its desires; and they often obeyed it at the cost of blood—causing their very limbs to be cut off if the dream so commended, and preparing solemn feasts for it. They offered sacrifices too, to their dream as to a divinity, and this by the advice of their diviners. They imagined that some people were more enlightened than others and capable of seeing into the depths of the soul where lay concealed its natural and most secret desires. These were commonly their Physicians or Charlatans, who when called to see a person, commonly used no other remedy except that of driving out the occult desire of the soul which was tormenting the patient's body.

The Hurons actually believed that there were three kinds of sickness. In addition to diseases caused by unconscious mental processes, the Hurons recognized diseases due to some natural causes, and curable with such things as herbs and poultices, and also diseases due to demonic possession, curable by shamanistic procedures.

The occurrence of these ideas about the unconscious mind among the Huron Indians raises two important questions: How did the Hurons come to have these ideas, ideas that were to be popularized some centuries later by disciples of Freud? And is there any evidence to indicate that these Huron ideas became known to European scholars of the seventeenth and subsequent centuries?

The Hurons were an extraordinary people, but our information about them is limited because they began to be wiped out even before the Jesuits came to know them. When first encountered, they occupied the St. Lawrence valley and the land north of Lake Ontario, but they soon became extinct in the St. Lawrence area. To the north, east, and west were Algonquian tribes. To the south, in New York State and the adjacent area of western Vermont, were the Iroquois. Authorities agree that the Hurons and the Iroquois were related, at least linguistically (2, 3). However, the Iroquois were relentless enemies of the Hurons, and were in the process of invading the

RELATION-ABRÉGÉE

QUELQUES MISSIONS
DES
Pères de la Comp.ie de Jésus
DANS LA NOUVELLE FRANCE,
PAR LE
P.F.J.BRESSANI,
DE LA MÊME COMPAGNIE,
DÉDIÉE À
L'E.E.et R.R.Seigneur
CARDINAL DE LUCO

IHS

À MACÉRATA
1653.

Title page of the popular seventeenth-century summary of the Jesuit relations.

Huron lands and slaughtering or carrying off the inhabitants when the first European settlers arrived.

Champlain wrote about the Hurons and the Iroquois in a fragmentary fashion—he was more interested in the land than in the people—but he did state in 1609 that the two peoples had been at war a long time (4). Champlain's statement clearly negates the view advanced by Trigger (5) and Heidenreich (6) that the war between the two tribes was motivated by a desire to control the fur trade with the French (who had not yet arrived in Canada in search of furs). The earliest accounts of the Huron Indians are to be found in these writings by Champlain and in others by Lescarbot in 1609 (7), Sagard in 1632 (8), and Lafitau in 1724 (9). Lescarbot's account of the exploration of Canada by Cartier, Champlain, and himself refers to Labrador, Newfoundland, the Maritimes, and the region of the Gulf of St. Lawrence, and he also mentioned other parts of the New World. Lafitau, a Jesuit, also ranged over the New World in his writings. (Lescarbot was later imprisoned for writing a satire against the Jesuits.)

Gabriel Sagard was not a priest, but rather a lay brother of the Recollects, a reform group of the Franciscan Order of Friars Minor, who received their name because of their emphasis on meditation. He seems to have been a man of education. However, he had no great interest in civil matters, only in saving souls. He was in Canada for only fifteen months, beginning in June 1623 (the Jesuits arrived in Huronia in 1625). According to Sagard the Hurons had a way of life completely different from any of their neighbors. Sagard evidently admired the Hurons greatly, despite the fact that they were disgustingly filthy in person and in habits. The word Huron is derived from the French and means "unkempt." (The Indian name for the nation was *Wendet*, which became *Wyandot*, after the dispersion of the Huron nation.)

The Hurons' behavior was perhaps a result of their desire not to have unsatisfied unconscious wishes. They shared everything, and what was not shared was likely to be stolen, especially if it was something owned by a stranger. Thievery was not punished, nor was anything else. After dark the young women prowled the villages in search of sexual partners. (The Hurons lived in settled villages, and lived mainly by agriculture and fishing.) All the children were treated alike, with complete solicitude. If a couple had too many children to take care of, others in the village would take them in and treat them as their own. No decisions of the chiefs and the governing councils could ever be enforced; they were put into effect only by begging the population to obey. Despite all this the people were often melancholic. Their extremely polite behavior did not keep them from being indifferent to the revolting impression they made on others. Many of the young men were not enthusiastic about warfare, and neither public opinion nor law could make them serve. On the other hand, some of them were recklessly brave. In their expeditions against the Iroquois they usually enlisted the aid of nearby Indian tribes or of the French, the latter armed with guns. Lescarbot said, "They will venture anywhere if backed by a band of Frenchmen." In his account of a joint expedition against the Iroquois in 1615, Champlain wrote:

> ...the chiefs have in fact no absolute control over their men, who are governed by their own will and follow their own fancy, which is the cause of their disorder and the ruin of all their undertakings; for, having determined upon anything with their leaders, it needs only the whim of a villain, or nothing at all, to lead them to break it off and form a new plan. Thus there is no concert of action among them, as can be seen by this expedition.

This way of doing things eventually led to the massacre of the nation and the ultimate disappearance of the survivors. (Eight Jesuit missionaries to the Hurons were also killed.) According to Lescarbot, their wars were "carried on solely by surprises, in the dead of night, or by ambushes, or subtlety." (They became more venturesome when accompanied by armed Frenchmen.) They often sent groups of up to a half-dozen to infiltrate the country of their neighbors, both enemy (the Iroquois) and neutral, for the purpose of capturing and bringing back one or two of them, dead or alive. If the captive was a man, he was tortured slowly until he died, the Hurons looking on happily. Many captives were eaten, also happily.

The Iroquois, a notably irritable people, did not consider these acts friendly. They killed many Hurons on sight, captured and tortured many more, and finally, their patience exhausted, they undertook an organized military campaign that wiped them out in 1649. This occurred despite the military aid from the French, which had begun as early as 1609. The Iroquois accordingly allied themselves with the English. Etienne Brulé, Champlain's emissary to the Hurons, was believed to be secretly serving the British, and in 1623 the Hurons ate him. Twenty-six years later there was no more Huron nation. The military disasters of the Hurons are best summarized by Parkman (10).

However, as Snyderman (11) has shown, the Six Nations adopted or otherwise incorporated large numbers of captured enemies, and even whole peoples. In fact, this policy was "in large measure responsible for the dominance of the Iroquois." In the seventeenth century Erie, Neutral, Huron, and Conestoga captives were incorporated. In 1748 the Senecas invited the Wyandots to join them. The Wyandots were of course the Hurons who had escaped the massacres a century earlier by moving to Kansas, Nebraska, and Oklahoma. Delaware and Shawnee groups were also brought in. In fact, the Iroquois confederation, the Six Nations, was originally the Five Nations, becoming six only with the incorporation of the Tuscaroras. An unknown number of Hurons joined Iroquois tribes in the New York State area. A few hundred Hurons remained in Canada under the protection of the French, with whom they inter married. A large number of Hurons escaped down the Mississippi Valley, and settled in Kansas, Nebraska and Oklahoma as the Wyandots. The records indicate that at first they were Roman Catholics; many wore silver crucifixes. However, in the nineteenth century they were all Methodists.

Trigger (5) and Heidenreich (6) believe that the actions of the Iroquois against the Hurons were commercially motivated, the prize being the control of the St. Lawrence valley fur trade. This modern interpretation of the economic basis of history may result from a confusion of cause and effect. Actually Lescarbot, three hundred years earlier, said:

Our savages do not found their wars upon the possession of land. We do not see that they encroach one upon another in that respect. They have land enough to live on and to walk abroad. Their ambition is limited by their bounds. They make war as did Alexander the Great, that they may say "I have beaten you"; or else for revenge, in remembrance of some injury received, which is the greatest vice I find in them, because they never forget injuries; wherein they are the more excusable, in that they do nothing but what we ourselves do also. They follow nature; and if we curb anything of that instinct, it is the commandment of God which makes us do so, whereunto many stop their eyes.

Evidently Lescarbot believed that as non-Christians, they should be forgiven all.

Before they vanished as a nation, the Hurons made a remarkable impression on European observers, an impression that was restated again and again. One of the earliest and best-known comments was by Sagard in his *Histoire du Canada*: "They are . . . like the nobility of a country. The Algonquian nations comprise the bourgeoisie; the peasants and poor are represented by Montagnais."

The Hurons maintained a life of self-indulgence, or, as it is described today, self-expression. The Iroquois lived a life of consideration for and service to the group. Although far from home, the Iroquois were able to live, while the Hurons were starving in their own land; the Iroquois were able to conduct military operations that wiped out the Hurons, leaving us today with many mysteries, among them the origin of the Huron ideas about the unconscious mind.

How had the Huron Indians acquired or developed the idea that unconscious thoughts, feelings, or emotions might cause diseases of many kinds? Had the idea arisen *de novo*, or had it been borrowed? If borrowed, had the Huron ideas come from the dreamlore and philosophies of other peoples and other times in the past? Such books as Ferm's *Primitive Religions*, Ratcliff's *A History of Dreams* and Wood's *The World of Dreams* gave no hint of any idea similar to that of the Hurons we are discussing here. The medicine of other primitive peoples was entirely shamanistic, that is, based on the invasion of the body by evil spirits which had to be persuaded to leave by being frightened or beaten, or perhaps by being enticed away. For the most part among primitive peoples, dreams were a device for getting together with one's ancestors, or with other friendly spirits, who advised, admonished, or perhaps scolded the dreamer. In a few instances reference may be found to the dream as wish fulfillment, usually involving some forbidden desire. The dreamer of such a dream was as guilty as if he had actually performed the antisocial act. Dreams were also important as prophecies, but these did not involve illness in a majority of instances and in any case the prophetic content of a dream required the interpretation of an expert. There is no indication that the Hurons had received their culture from a more civilized source then themselves. Certainly the psychologies of ancient Indian and Mediterranean cultures bear little or no resemblance to the Huron ideas. It is true that the psychology of Plato and his followers refers to dreams as wish fulfillment, as Rand's *The Classical Psychologists* (12) and Watson's *The Great Psychologists* show (13). However, this is different from the Huron's ideas of unconscious processes as the cause of disease.

In the absence of any evidence in remote primitive or ancient peoples of medical beliefs similar to those of the Hurons, one must consider the possibility that they might have existed in the area as a whole. However, medicine among their Algonquian neighbors, like medicine among other American Indian peoples and their presumed ancestors, the Siberians, was entirely shamanistic and included no belief similar to the Hurons' respecting the medical importance of the unconscious mind. Lescarbot does mention an instance in which members of an Algonquian tribe, the Montagnais, expressed an idea similar to that of the Hurons on unconscious thinking. In a fight between eleven Montagnais and the Iroquois, one Montagnais was wounded. "If he dreamt anything," Lescarbot said, "all the ten others were forced to carry it out to content him, believing also that his hurt would be better thereby." (It should be noted that by this date—1623—the Montagnais had long been warrior allies of the Hurons.)

As Blau (14) and others have shown, the seventeenth-century ideas about the unconscious mind held by the Hurons may be found, albeit less strongly emphasized, in beliefs held today, three hundred years later, by various Iroquois peoples (e.g., Onondagas, Ontario Iroquois, Tonawanda Senecas, and Cayugas). This is exemplified by the Mid-Winter Feast, a dream-guessing ceremony, used by both the Hurons and the Iroquois, and still practiced by the Iroquois today. However, it appears to be a mechanism for giving wanted gifts at midwinter—much like Chanukah and Christmas today—and not an explanation of the cause and treatment of illnesses. Lafitau (9) recognized the distinction between this ceremony and ideas about disease. It is impossible to state whether all the Iroquois peoples listed above held these beliefs as early as did the Hurons, but a pertinent reference to an Onondaga statement in 1656 does exist (14). This, however, tells us nothing about who held the ideas first, because it is clear that the Hurons had by then largely disappeared, many of them into Iroquois tribes. Hence it is possible that Huron ideas about the unconscious mind entered Iroquois thinking in that fashion. On the other hand, the ideas of both the Hurons and the Iroquois may have a common earlier source. The linguistic relations of the Huron and Iroquois languages suggest that the two peoples had once been closely related.

Wallace (15, 16) has published two curious articles that purport to describe the unconscious thinking of the Iroquois. These writings are defective in several ways. For one thing he does not justify his failure to note that he is talking about today's Iroquois and not those of three centuries ago. Moreover, he regards seventeenth-century Huron ideas as an expression of Iroquois thinking. These scholarly deficiencies are compounded by his interpretation of selected Iroquois material in the stereotyped manner typical of Freudian dogma. Before accepting these clichés, the reader might want to make a study of comparable stereotypes, by examining the clichés used by an Indian interpreting a white man's dreams (17). Wallace's writings do not apply to the problems of our present discussion.

Another way of gaining information bearing on our problem is to study the lore of the Wyandot Indians of the Mississippi Valley, because they are believed to represent parts of the Huron nation that had escaped being killed or absorbed by the Iroquois. However, the writings about these peoples (18, 19) contain no references to the Huron ideas under consideration here—they had been lost en route.

In the absence of definitive information about the origin of Huron ideas about the unconscious, one must consider other possibilities. Did the Indians of eastern Canada have enough contact with Norsemen, before the arrival of the French, to have gotten the ideas from them? We know that there were contacts for a number of years. Battles between the two have been pictured, and the Indians' weapons are clearly Algonquian. Even though the Norse could not establish successful settlements on continental America, they did trade with the natives, at least for several centuries (20). The wood used for houses in Greenland must have come from America. However extant Icelandic medical manuscripts make no mention of anything resembling Huron ideas. By the thirteenth century Icelandic medicine seems to have become a version of that of the school of Salerno (21). This does not preclude the possibility of an indigenous verbal medical tradition different from written medicine in Iceland, the indigenous elements having become lost in the wave of great new medicine from Salerno. But the sagas contain no mention of ideas similar to those of the Hurons, and hence this entire idea is best abandoned.

Another possibility is that the Huron-Iroquois people brought the idea with them when they migrated into New York State and Southeastern Canada from some unknown areas to the south. They appear to have come up the Ohio Valley, but from where? Is it significant that the remnants of the Hurons settled in the Kansas-Nebraska area after being driven out of Canada? Recent archeological evidence suggests that a people whose villages resembled those of the Hurons had lived to the west and south but had been driven out by invaders from the west (22). The Hurons entered lands that had been held by Algonquian tribes at least as early as the tenth century. The Huron tribes—numbering between four and six—were distinctive in that they were friendly to and cooperated with the Algonquins (23) whereas the Iroquois maintained a constant state of war with them. Yet this did not preclude the absorption into the New York State Iroquois of large numbers of Algonquian and Huron groups.

At the moment the best conclusion seems to be that the Huron Indians brought their ideas about the unconscious mind with them when they came to Canada.

The ideas discussed here are so strikingly similar to some

that are believed to have originated in Vienna less than a century ago that one wonders if the Huron ideas could have influenced European (and later, American) thinking on the subject. We have no certain answer to that question either, and the evidence is at best only suggestive. Therefore, let us pass immediately to the mid-nineteenth century in Europe.

By then the idea of reflexes, which were unconscious, had become established after the works of Whytt a hundred years earlier. Some physicians, including Laycock of Edinborough, believed that all thought was reflex. Laycock was among those who stated that childhood events might determine the nature of hysterical symptoms occurring later in life. The nineteenth century was an era of introspective psychology, and all psychologists who wrote during that period discussed with different degrees of thoroughness the phenomenon of unconscious thought. In Germany, Beneke and Herbart had pointed out that the same thoughts might enter and leave consciousness and that therefore they must exist in some unconscious form. Many authors discussed repression of ideas below the threshold of consciousness. This, they said, was particularly likely to occur when the ideas in a person's mind were in conflict. Herbart's many writings, first published in the early 1800s and republished in several editions up to 1891, contained many pages on the subject. Some of these works were still in common use in the twentieth century.

It is difficult—or perhaps impossible—to find a nineteenth-century psychologist or medical psychologist who did not recognize unconscious cerebration not only as real but of the highest importance. One curious result of nineteenth-century interest in the unconscious was Creighton's book (24), in which he expressed his belief that many bodily diseases are caused by unconscious mental processes. His theories referred to habits that had become unconscious but that continued to exert their effects, causing physiologic disturbances and hence diseases. One exception to this general scheme was Creighton's explanation of how cancer originated. In his view it was the result of a cell in an adult body having unconscious memories of its embryonic state!

We can now appreciate that the late nineteenth century saw

the acceptance of ideas about the unconscious mind that were both perceptive and extensive. The twentieth century has added little.

Why did these ideas arise and develop so rapidly at that time? We cannot explain this phenomenon with certainty, but there are some strong indications that should be investigated. Let us consider the intellectual atmosphere of the eighteenth century. The writings of seventeenth-century travelers in Africa and America had led to a rebirth of the ancient myth of the noble savage. In the eighteenth century Rousseau's writings stated emphatically that civilization was a social disease, and that only the uncivilized were noble. His ideas created a great controversy. The bitterness with which they were attacked can be appreciated only by reading the criticism. Probably the most persistent, vocal, and bitter critic was Buffon, the famous naturalist. In his writings he stated that the American Indian was a degenerate, that he was sexually inferior (as evidenced by his lack of a beard), that Europeans who came to live in America degenerated (with no mention of the beards), that American animals were degenerated, that European animals taken to America degenerated and did not multiply, and so on. The writings of Buffon and others like him were answered by men, among them Chateaubriand (25), who tried to prove that the noble savage was a real person, the real product of a favorable environment. Why then did Chateaubriand, who had actually visited Canada, not note the remarkable Huron ideas? One answer is that there was by then no longer a Huron culture. Another answer is that Chateaubriand appears to have been too romantic a commentator to have paid attention to any weighty ideas that he might have stumbled on.

The battle between the followers of Rousseau and those of Buffon raged for decades. Some ammunition for the former was found in the popular writings of Sagard and more particularly in those of Lafitau, who, it will be remembered, did refer to the Huron's ideas about the effects of unconscious thinking. It is difficult to find specific references in learned works of the seventeenth and eighteenth centuries to material contained in the Jesuit writings. It was not customary for the intellectuals of these centuries to mention in their writings the names of any but the most famous scholars of the past. Nevertheless, it must be taken for granted that the Jesuit materials were used. For example, it is interesting to note that the libretto of Mozart's *Die Zauberflöte*, seemingly a nonsensical mixture of ancient Egyptian and seventeenth-century American Indian lore, becomes reasonable only if one assumes that its author had been influenced by some book such as Lafitau's.

It is probable that the contents of the *Jesuit Relations* provided ammunition in this battle. Not only were these reports complete and detailed eyewitness accounts but they actually were about noble savages, the Huron Indians.

The *Jesuit Relations* were widely read. They were published annually in Paris by Sébastien and Gabriel Cramoisy in the seventeenth century. These reports and related documents became important sources of information about Canada in the seventeenth and subsequent centuries. They were used by Bancroft for his *History of the United States of America* (26) by Sparks for his *American Biography* (27), and by Parkman in several of his works (10, 28). Father Bressani, one of the Jesuit missionaries, wrote his condensed version of the *Relations* in Italian in 1673, evidently in response to popular demand. This work was later translated into French (29). The *Jesuit Relations* were also later used in many scholarly writings not for the general public. The *Jesuit Relations* plus additional documents were republished by the Canadian government in 1858, and the English edition was published in Cleveland in 1898 (1).

It is evident that scholars and intelligent laypersons had read about the Huron Indians by the mid-nineteenth century. Did these readers include psychologists and psychiatrists of the eighteenth and nineteenth centuries? The answer is probably affirmative. Did some of these readers accept and use the Hurons' ideas about the unconscious mind, perhaps without knowing their source? The answer can, at the moment, be only a weak and tentative yes. One alternative is to consider the rise of ideas about unconscious thinking during or before the sixteenth century in Canada, and in the nineteenth century in Europe, an example of parallel, if not simultaneous, development. If such parallel development did indeed take place, there is no way to prove it. Occurrences of this sort are assumed proved if no evidence is found to prove some other mechanism. Of course, proof of this sort is no proof at all, although it is customarily advanced as if it were by advocates of the collective-mind concept, accepted as a reality by ancient Greek philosophers, medieval theologians, some modern psychologists of the more mystic variety, and by psychoanalysts. Acceptance of this dubious but romantic notion would require, among other things, that we believe that the weird plot of Mozart's *Magic Flute* and the contents of Lafitau's book had been locked since the beginning of time in the filing cabinet of the collective mind, to be brought forth by the two men in the eighteenth century. I doubt that many will accept this explanation of the coincidence.

It is clear that our inquiry into possible relations between Huron and later European ideas about an unconscious mind has yielded little of substance. This is perhaps disappointing, but not excessively so, for this has been the first time the inquiry has been made.

REFERENCES

1. Ragueneau, P. Relation de ce que s'est passé dans la Mission des Pères de la Compagnie de Jesus aux Hurons pays de la Nouvelle France, des années 1647 et 1648. In *The Jesuit relations and allied documents. Travels and explorations of the Jesuit missionaires in New France. 1610-1791.* Vol. 33. R. Gold Thwaites, ed. Cleveland: Burrows Brothers, 1898, p. 59.

2. Maclean, J. *Canadian savage folk: The native tribes of Canada.* Toronto: W. Briggs, 1896.

3. Jenness, E. *The Indian tribes of Canada.* Toronto: Ryerson Press, 1933, pp. 20 ff.

4. Laverdierre, C.-H. *Oeuvres de Champlain, publiées sous le patronage de l'Université Laval.* 2nd ed. Quebec: G.-E. Desbarats, 1870. Chapter 7 of 1607 ed.

5. Trigger, B. G. Trade and tribal warfare on the St. Lawrence in the sixteenth century. *Ethnology* 9:240-256, 1962.

6. Heidenreich, C. *Huronia: A history of geography of the Huron Indians, 1600-1650.* Ontario Ministry of Natural Resources, Historical Sites Branch, 1971.

7. Lescarbot, M. *The history of New France.* W. L. Grant, trans. Toronto: Champlain Society, 1907.

8. Sagard, F. G. *Histoire du Canada. The long journey to the country of the Hurons.* G. M. Wrong, ed. H. H. Langton, trans. Toronto: Champlain Society, 1939.

9. Lafitau, J. F. *Moeurs des sauvages Américaines, comparé aux moeurs des premiers temps.* Paris: S. R. Saugrain and C. E. Hochereau, 1724.
10. Parkman, F. *France and England in North America.* Boston: Little, Brown, 1878.
11. Snyderman, G. S. Concepts of land ownership among the Iroquois and their neighbors. In *Symposium on local diversity in Iroquois culture.* W. N. Fenton, ed. Smithsonian Institution. *Bulletin of American Ethnology,* Bulletin 149, 1951.
12. Rand, B. *The classical psychologists.* Boston: Houghton Mifflin, 1912.
13. Watson, R. L. *The great psychologists.* Philadelphia: Lippincott, 1963.
14. Blau, H. Dream guessing: A comparative analysis. *Ethnohistory* 10:233, 1963.
15. Wallace, A. F. C. The institutionalization of cathartic and control studies in Iroquois religious psychotherapy. In *Culture and Mental Health.* M. K. Opler, ed. New York: Macmillan, 1959.
16. Wallace, A. F. C. Psychoanalysis among the Iroquois of New York State. In *The Americas on the eve of discovery.* H. E. Driver, ed. Englewood Cliffs, N.J.: Prentice-Hall, 1964.
17. Lincoln, J. S. A Navajo Indian medicine man interprets a white man's dream. In *The world of dreams.* R. L. Woods, ed. New York: Random House, 1947.
18. Finley, J. B. *History of the Wyandot mission at Upper Sandusky, Ohio.* Cincinnati: J. F. Wright & L. Swarmstedt, 1840.
19. Connelly, W. E. *Wyandot folk-lore.* Topeka, Kans.: Crane, 1899.
20. Arbman, H. *The Vikings.* New York: Praeger, 1961, pp. 115 ff.
21. Larsen, H. An old Icelandic medical manuscript. *Annals of Medical History* 9:60, 1927.
22. Libassi, P. T. The 10,000-year deep dig. *The Sciences,* May–June, 1975, p. 15.
23. Orr, R. B. *The Iroquois in Canada.* Thirty-First Archeological Report of the Minister of Education. Toronto: A. T. Wilgress, 1919.
24. Creighton, C. *Illustration of unconscious memory in disease, including a theory of alteratives.* New York: Vail, 1886.
25. Chateaubriand, F.-R. *Oeuvres romanesques et voyages.* M. Regard, ed. Paris: Gallimard, 1969.
26. Bancroft G. *History of the United States of America: From the discovery of the continent to 1885.* Abr. ed. Chicago: University of Chicago Press, 1966.
27. Sparks, J. *The Library of American Biography.* Boston: Hilliard, Gray, 1834–1848.
28. Parkman, F. *The Jesuits in North America in the seventeenth century.* Boston: Little, Brown, 1902.
29. Bressani, F. G. *Breve relatione d'Alcune Missioni de' P.P. della Compagnia di Giesu nella Nova Francia.* Macerata, Italy: Heredi d'Agostino Grisei, 1653.

Chapter 3

ST. ISIDORE OF SEVILLE
and his depressing ideas
about depression

Two imaginary representations of St. Isidore of Seville (left) in a tenth-century manuscript and (right) in an eighteenth-century oil painting by an unknown Spanish artist.

Isidore, Archbishop of Seville in the seventh century, is well known for his role in the preservation of learning in the West after the collapse of the Roman Empire. He did not merely transmit what was available to him. He analyzed it, synthesized its significant contents, and presented it as one organized system of information, belief, and learned opinion as it then existed. However, the significance of some of his writings has never been fully appreciated. This applies particularly to some of his more original writings and particularly to one of them, the *Synonyma*. This work is highly important in the history of psychiatry because part of it is the earliest recorded first-person account of a delusional (psychotic) depression.

The circumstances in which the *Synonyma* was written require analysis. What is known about Isidore's background is that his family had resided in Cartagena for some time before moving to Seville. Cartagena had been founded centuries earlier as New Carthage, a Phoenician colony, part of the expanding commercial empire of that Semitic people. However, there is nothing to indicate a Semitic origin of the family; all the recorded family names in the sixth and seventh centuries are Roman. The family were devout Catholics. The conquest of Spain by the Visigoths had evidently caused the family little inconvenience, for although the Visigoths were Arian heretics, they did not seriously interfere with the Roman Catholic church in Spain. However, when the Emperor Justinian's Byzantine forces conquered the southern coast of Spain, the newly imposed rule by the heretic Hellenized Romans evidently was sufficiently troubling to the family to make them move to Seville, a strongly Catholic city to the northwest. Isidore was born in that city, but he never lost his dislike of the Byzantines. When a Visigoth army finally forced the surrender of the last Byzantine forces in Spain, Isidore wrote with such exuberant satisfaction about the defeat of the "Romans," as he called them, that some modern authors have concluded that Isidore must have been a Visigoth himself. It must be remembered, however, that after the fall of Rome, all the eastern Mediterranean peoples called Constantinople "the second Rome" (just as the later fall of Constantinople led the Russians to call Moscow "the third Rome"). In fact, the Byzantine empire was long called *Rum*. The Romans in Isidore's letter were Hellenized East Romans.

Isidore's family had a remarkable record. His brother, Leander, was Catholic Archbishop of Seville. After Leander's death, Isidore was chosen for that post.* The only other brother was bishop in a smaller diocese in Spain. The only sister became a nun. When the Visigothic king decided, in the interest of national unity, to give up his Arian heresy and adopt the Catholic faith, the religious reorganization of the country was led by Isidore. He carried it out successfully, and he became the confidant and advisor of the king for the rest of his life. In addition to being an effective leader and administrator during a time of crisis in the early Catholic Church in Spain, Isidore was one of the leading scholars, and his organized account of the pagan and Christian learning of an era that was falling into disorder and decay became a standard source for scholars of the Christian West for many centuries. Together with such other churchmen as the Venerable Bede, and such laymen as Cassiodorus, he ranks high among the preservers of Roman culture after the collapse of the Empire. As Castro (1) has emphasized,

---

*Some early writers state or imply that Isidore was a Benedictine monk, or, if not a monk, an abbot of a Benedictine monastery. The evidence against these notions is presented by Julio Pérez Llamazares, ¿San Isidoro de Sevilla, Monje? In *Homenaje a S. Isidoro de Sevilla en el XII Centenario de su Muerte*. La Provincia de Andalucía S. I., ed. Rome: Press of the Pontifical Gregorian University, 1936.

Isidore's organized, ordered presentation of what was known in his time was peculiarly satisfying to the Occidental mind, and remained so for centuries. For example, a catalogue of heresies written years later in the sixteenth century still contained material from Isidore's writings (2). Theologians were not the only scholars who were indebted to Isidore. A recent account of medieval biology by Rowland (3) has many references to Isidore's writings. Others who were indebted to Isidore included the late-medieval poets Gower and Lydgate, disciples of Chaucer; they owned and used Isidore's writings, as the *Dictionary of National Biography* makes clear. Likewise, as MacKinney (4) pointed out, medieval physicians often used Isidore's works; his medical writings, as discussed by Sharpe (5), are clearly recognizable as a source of the ideas held by other physicians of that era. Castro (1), in agreement with other authorities, emphasized that the rapid, widespread, and lasting diffusion of Isidore's works was one of the most notable phenomena in the history of Western culture.

Today, however, many scholars consider Isidore a mere compiler of ancient misinformation, because in the light of present scientific knowledge his descriptions of the natural world, in his *Etymologia*, are at best trivial and at worst downright silly. Although this view of Isidore's insignificance is valid for today's science, it is misleading in that it submerges his original contributions in a number of areas, and his historical importance in some others. It cannot be said that Isidore had no originality at all. On the contrary, evidence of Isidore's critical ability was shown early, for example, in his comment about the work of Falconia Proba, a lady poet who achieved fame with a poem composed of snippets taken entirely from Virgil. As Rand (6) noted, Isidore politely wrote, "We do not like the idea, but cannot keep admiring the author's ingenuity." Actually Isidore made original contributions in a more important sector. As Endres (7) showed convincingly, Isidore was a pioneer in the development of the Scholastic method that characterized medieval philosophy and reached its peak in the *Summa Theologiae* of Thomas Aquinas. Isidore's role in the creation of a philosophical method that was basic to all of medieval Christian thought would be enough by itself to guarantee his immortality in the history of scholarship. His importance in other aspects of history is also great but not pertinent to the present discussion except for one item: he wrote the earliest recorded first-person account of a delusional (endogenous, psychotic) depression. Since it is evident that Isidore was an intelligent, well-organized thinker, both as a scholar and as an administrator, it is important to learn how he became able to describe accurately the thoughts and feelings he experienced during that kind of depression. In the *Synonyma* he wrote (8):

My soul is in affliction, my spirit is troubled, my heart trembles, distress of soul afflicts me. Distress of the spirit afflicts me, I am surrounded by all evils, encompassed by bitterness, enclosed by mischance, besieged with misery, covered with unhappiness, weighed down by troubles; I find no reason for such great sorrow, I do not understand how to escape adversity, I cannot find a way to escape grief. I cannot find ways of decreasing my sorrow, everywhere my unhappiness pursues me, at home or outside, my calamity is always with me.

Wherever I flee, my evils pursue me; wherever I turn, the shadow of my woes accompanies me like the shadow of my body. Hence I cannot flee my own ill luck. I am a man of unknown name, of obscure opinion, of humble lineage, known by myself only. I have harmed no one; I have maligned no one; I have stood against no one; I have brought trouble on no one, and disturbed no one, I have lived among men without any complaint. All gnash and rage against me, drag me to destruction, lead me to danger, attack my safety. No one gives me protection, no one takes on my defense, no one gives me support, no one relieves my woes. I am deserted by all men. Those who look at me either flee, or else they pursue me. They look upon me as an unhappy man, and falsely say I know not what with comforting words. They hide their hidden malice with bland words, and speak one thing with their mouths and intend another in their hearts. By their deeds they destroy what they promised with their mouths. Under the guise of pity they exult over the injured heart.

They cloak malice with the disguise of goodness; they conceal craftiness with false simplicity, they feign friendship by guile; they show in their face what they do not carry in their heart. In whom may you believe? In whom may you put faith? Whom will you consider your neighbor? Where now is faith?

Faith has perished, has been driven away, it is nowhere safe. If nothing is honest, if there is no truth of judgment, if decency is abandoned, if law is not maintained, if justice is denied to all, then laws perish, and chance becomes the judge.

Avarice has grown. The law perishes because of love of greed. Laws have no power; gifts and bribes have taken the strength from the laws.

Everywhere money conquers; everywhere judgment is for sale. There is no fear of the law, no dread of judgment. License to live wickedly goes unpunished; no one opposes the sinners, nor is any misdeed punished. All crime remains unavenged: the wicked are saved: the innocent die. The good are needy: the evil are wealthy: criminals are powerful.

The just are in need; wrongdoers are honored; the just are despised. The wrongdoers rejoice; the just are in sorrow and grief. The wicked man prevails against the righteous. The evil condemn the good. The bad man is honored instead of a good man, the good man condemned instead of an evil one; the innocent perish instead of the guilty, and nothing stops it.

For no reason, without complaint, or malice on my part, they accuse me of crime. They heap crime on me: they weave the snares of crime against me. They impute crime and suspicion to me. They lead me into wrongdoing and danger: they cast crime on me, of which I have no knowledge. Nothing was sought for nothing was revealed, no inquiry was made, nothing was found, and yet they continue to contrive evils against me. They ceaselessly prepare false testimonies. My accusers do not stop accusing, but the judge does not put it in writing.

I am condemned by the false and malicious opinions of witnesses and judges. By the false testimony of witnesses, I, though innocent, am led to death. The witnesses and judges are involved in the same plot, my accusers the same group. They present wicked judges; they bring forth false witnesses, in whose testimony they trust. No one dissents from them, no one disagrees, no one repudiates their counsel. To whom may I speak? Whom may I believe? Whom may I petition? To whom may I go? From whom may I seek counsel? In whose hands shall I place my soul? What protector shall I seek?

I am hateful to all, deserted by the love of all. All have cast me from them, regard me with abomination. All shudder at me, repudiate me, want to desert me. I wish to flee them not, but they threaten me. I desire to pray at their footsteps, but they flee, turn their backs and hate me. I want to make them favorable with my pleadings, but they become all the more annoyed. Meanwhile they approach me with feigned love, not for to give consolation but to tempt me. They speak falsely, and if they are silent, it is not a sincere silence. They seek for something to accuse me with, something to hear, something to bring out, to seek causes for deception.

But I, with hanging head, cast-down visage and lowered face, am silent, am dumb, and remain in ashamed silence. I set a guard and a seal on my mouth. I restrained my voice from speaking, I held back my tongue from talking. Even when asked about good I am silent, for I preferred to remain silent to evil folk, rather than to answer. But they were not quiet: they raged all the more. They persecute me, already shaken even more. They attack me more and more, they cry out in rage against me. They aggressively deliver accusations with voice, gesture and shouting.

They leap forth onto me, with a public outcry. They hurl contumely and reproaches at me, and they all, encouraged by another, rush toward me, and turn their weapons on me. They all rage at me, they strive for my destruction, they ready their hands for my death. Therefore, in such great fear, terror and fright, wretched, I melted, grew pale, and became bloodless. My heart fainted. I am agitated with fear, I melt with the terror of my fright. Fear and trembling have shaken my soul.

Thus I am thrust into and condemned to exile, thus I suffer the penalty of exile, thus I groan because of the condemnation of exile, led in the chain of slavery, crushed by the burden of my condition, enslaved with menial work, in chill weather, in snow, in cold, in raging storms, forced into every task, in every danger. After the condemning of my goods, after the loss of all my possessions, I am made poor and needy. I lack, I beg unhappily, I publicly implore alms. No one stretches out his hand to the needy, no one helps the poor. I am not considered worthy of anyone's pity, I am deprived of everyone's mercy. There is no one who will have pity.

All scorn the beggar, and do not restore the needy with their crumbs. No one pours a refreshing drop into the mouth of the thirsty. No one offers me even a moderate dew-drop of water, for I am made hateful to all. Whenever anyone looks upon me, all despise me as if I were covered with sores, reject me as full of sores, shudder to touch me as if I were a leper. My body is restrained by irons, held by chains, bound by fetters, confined by bonds. The torture, the torments, the punishment do not cease for me. Their fierceness is cruel to me continually.

The butchers rend me with new bodily torture, they tear my insides and limbs with unheard-of kinds of punishment, they invent whatever cruelty they can against me. I do not die a simple death, but am tortured by a thousand pains, a thousand tortures, a thousand punishments. My flesh has festered, slashed with wounds. My half-burned sides pour out pus, my torn limbs drip with stench, blood flows in my tears, and gore in my weeping. It is not only a weeping of tears, but of wounds.

I am wretched, I am consumed with sorrow, my soul is in anguish, and my body fails. Finally my mind is conquered, my soul is shackled with sorrow. I have experienced much that is unbearable, bitter and heavy. So serious and cruel a wound I have never received. I am burdened with an unthinkable wound, I am threatened with death every moment. An unexpected calamity crushed me unaware, sudden destructions and misfortunes fell on me.

Unhappy that I am, why was I born? Why was I thrust into this miserable life? Why did I, a pitiable man, ever see the light of day? Why did the beginning of this life happen to me? Would that I might depart more swiftly from this world than I entered it. With good reason now would I go! But alas! Longed-for death comes slowly to the wretched. Let the one who desires to die succumb. For I am weary of living. I desire to die, death alone pleases me. O death, how soothing you are to the wretched! O death, how sweet you are to those who live in bitterness! How cheering you are, O death, to the sorrowful and grieving!

Therefore let the great solace of death follow the great evil of life: let the end of life be the finish of such great evils: let the repose of the sepulchre bring an end to misery: and if life will not, let death at least begin to have pity. Death brings an end to all evils, affords a conclusion to calamity, destroys all misfortune. But, surely death helps the wretched. It is better to die well than to live wretchedly; it is better not to exist than to exist unhappily. This is clear from the magnitude of my sorrows. I bewail that I am stricken, I weep at my calamity, I grieve because of the inseparable pain of my misery. Wretched, I cannot be consoled; my sorrow is unremitting, my grief is endless. My wound is not bound up; there is no moderating of my tears, no end to my sorrows. Now there is no hope of soul. Now the soul cannot endure. Now the soul falls, overcome with miseries.

Some authors who have discussed these words consider them as nothing but an extended paraphrase of those of others. For example in Job 3, we find:

2. And Job spake, and said.
3. Let the day perish wherein I was born, and the night in which it was said, There is a man child conceived.
4. Let that day be darkness: let not God regard it from above, neither let the light shine upon it.
5. Let darkness and the shadow of death stain it; let a cloud dwell upon it; let the blackness of the day terrify it.
6. As for that night, let darkness seize upon it: let it not be joined unto the days of the year, let it not come into the number of the months.
7. Lo, let that night be solitary, let no joyful voice come therein.
8. Let them curse it that curse the day, who are ready to raise up their mourning.
9. Let the stars of the twilight thereof be dark; let it look for light, but have none; neither let it see the dawning of the day;

However this is clearly different from Isidore's situation; unlike Isidore, Job has ample cause for his depressed feelings, as we see in Job 1:

14. And there came a messenger unto Job, and said, The oxen were plowing, and the asses feeding beside them:
15. And the Sabeans fell *upon them*, and took them away; yea, they have slain the servants with the edge of the sword; and I only am escaped alone to tell thee.
16. While he was yet speaking, there came also another, and said, The fire of God is fallen from heaven, and hath burned up the sheep, and the servants, and consumed them; and I only am escaped alone to tell thee.

17. While he was yet speaking, there came also another, and said, The Chaldeans made out three bands, and fell upon the camels, and have carried them away, yea, and slain the servants with the edge of the sword; and I only am escaped alone to tell thee.

18. While he was yet speaking, there came also another, and said, Thy sons and thy daughters were eating and drinking wine in their eldest brother's house:

19. And, behold, there came a great wind from the wilderness, and smote the four corners of the house, and it fell upon the young men, and they are dead; and I only am escaped alone to tell thee.

Not only is any specific cause other than the vaguely referred to enemies absent from Isidore's writings, but there is in them a strong paranoid trend, of a typically puzzled, unsystematized, i.e., depressive, type that is not found in Job's words. Isidore's writing remains the first account of the thoughts and feelings of a person with a delusional depression.

The idea that the depression described by Isidore was endogenous, that is, without any known external cause, was not acceptable to medieval theologians or their modern followers. Sr. Patrick Mullins (9) makes this point strongly in her treatise (which is by far the best analysis of St. Isidore's thinking in fields other than science and medicine.) As Sister Mullins points out, Isidore introduced another character who discusses the depression with the one who was himself describing it. The depressed one becomes convinced that since he was being made to suffer, he must have sinned. He says later, "Alas, wretched and miserable that I am! I knew not that I was stricken for my own iniquity. I realized not that I was suffering for my own deserts." However, Mullins begs the question when she says that this disturbed and irrational type of mind proceeds from "inquietude of mind or despair of forgiveness" This confuses the manifestations of a psychiatric illness with its causes.

The idea of melancholy without a personal cause clearly did not appeal to Isidore, although one of his predecessors, Chrysostom, recognized it. Klibansky and his co-workers (10) discussed Chrysostom's letter, written around A.D. 380 to Stagirius, a depressed monk. In the letter, Chrysostom explained this kind of depression as being caused by the Devil, who was allowed by God to plague innocent men in order to test them.

Those who resisted the Fiend could expect to be rewarded richly on Judgment Day. Chrysostom held that his explanation made the depression not only understandable but tolerable: "You can overcome your depression if you say that you have done nothing to deserve it." In addition, according to Chrysostom, it was advisable to appeal to God's providence. However, most medieval authorities, including Isidore, continued to regard depression as punishment for sin. Much later, in the eighteenth century, a number of philosophers, including Kant, reasserted the medieval belief that depression came from a person's awareness of his own and other people's worthlessness. This explanation is best regarded today as an example of the failure to distinguish between the causes of a mental disorder and its manifestations—a mistake commonly encountered in modern psychiatric theory.

Some authors hold that Isidore wrote the *Synonyma* merely as a literary exercise designed to give him an opportunity to deploy all the consolatory clichés in his pedagogic armamentarium. Taylor (11) states this explicitly and Rigg (12) implies it. However, this view receives no support from the words of Isidore himself. In one letter to Archdeacon Braulio, Isidore mentions having completed his *Synonyma*, and adds "I am weak with infirmities of the flesh and with fault of mind. In both I ask your protection because I deserve nothing on my own merits" (13). This letter, whose date is given by de Aldama (14) as around A.D. 610-615, mentions depression not in response to a situational misfortune but as an irrational non sequitur to a happy accomplishment. In later letters (A.D. 632-633), also to Barulio, Isidore's tone is quite different, in that he makes vague mention of unspecified sins in what seems to be a perfunctorily traditional manner. Even stronger evidence that he experienced a depression of this type is found in the preface to the *Synonyma*, where Isidore says that his purpose is to "fashion a lament for myself or for the miserable." On the other hand, there is no need to assume that Isidore experienced all the thoughts and feelings he listed. He was, after all, a pedagogue in the Ciceronian tradition, and he might very well have amplified and extended his remarks with material he had read or had heard from others.

Leclercq and others (15) and Leclercq alone (16) have discussed the psychopathology of medieval Christian scholars and saints but have not discussed St. Isidore in this connection. Adnes (17) attempted a psychologic analysis of the saint and concluded, on the basis of fragmentary and largely irrelevant data combined with the trivial theories of Kretschmer (a famous psychiatrist of the twentieth century), that Isidore was a schizoid personality. All we can state today is that he had a delusional depression and seemed not to have any disorder of thinking.

Isidore's ideas about his own depression are difficult to characterize, for they are nowhere stated explicitly. Part of the problem arises from the fact that Isidore's various writings derive from two separate traditions. One is the tradition of the Roman encyclopedists, exemplified by Pliny and Celsus. Isidore's medical writings fall into this tradition. Medical writings of the period did little more than state the fact that melancholic patients have an abnormal mood and are likely to harbor delusions. Isidore's summary of previous writings on melancholia follow this pattern, as Sharpe's translation (5) shows. Since Isidore's medical writings were entirely derived, they contained no added material from his own experience. Moreover, Isidore had no experience as a medical practitioner and hence resembles the beginning student who glibly recites all that is known about a disease but cannot recognize it in a patient.

The second, and unrelated, tradition in which Isidore wrote was as a churchman. Half a dozen centuries later, these two traditions came together in the writing of Bartolomeus Anglicus, but in Isidore's time they were still separate. A medieval churchman's ideas about depression inevitably began with St. Paul. In his Second Epistle to the Corinthians 7:10, Paul wrote: "For godly sorrow worketh repentance to salvation not to be repented of, but the sorrow of the world worketh death." The word *sorrow*, as used in English translations of the Bible, stood for the *tristitia* of Latin versions, connoting sadness, sorrow, despondency, depression. Paul's distinction between the two kinds of *tristitia*, the one "from God" and the other "of the world" led medieval theologians to enlarge on differences between the two kinds of depression.

An early exegetist, the pre-Nicene father Origen (18) discussed the death of Judas Iscariot in the light of Paul's concepts. Origen held that although Judas's sin was not too great for forgiveness, his remorse was excessive (!) and the Devil was therefore able to direct him away from the beneficent depression that makes for penitence, and toward the depression that leads to death. In the minds of the early churchmen penitence was clearly the hallmark of the benign depression. (Today we call it insight.)

However, it was the perceptive psychologist John Cassian who began to give the discussion a modern psychiatric cast. His guide to the monastic life, *De Institutis Coenobiorum*, written around the year A.D. 420, included a discussion of how a monk could distinguish the two kinds of depression. The second kind, Cassian said, is rancorous, ineffective, and irrational. His ideas were repeated two centuries later by Isidore of Seville, who contrasted the "disturbed irrational" second type with the "temperate and rational" first type. Isidore clearly recognized the existence of disturbed irrational depressions, but he did not point out that his own had this character. This apparent mystery ceases to be one if we consider that Isidore's purpose is purely consolatory, as he himselfs states. In the *Synonyma* the consolation is offered by a person designated as Reason; it constitutes the second part of the work. In this sense the *Synonyma* is to be grouped with the consolatory writings, such as those of Cicero and St. Augustine, as Fontaine (19) and Rigg (12) observe.

However, the *Synonyma* differed from all previous consolatory writings in one important respect. Cicero's consolatory *Tusculan Disputations* refers to the value of suffering, including physical suffering, for improving the soul (20). Augustine's consolatory remarks are in a different category: his despondency and remorse were purely situational, and were in response to the sins he lists explicitly (and with great relish) (21). As one would expect of a reformed sinner, he found consolation for his despondency in repentance; his depression clearly showed itself to be rational and hence benign. Isidore's consolatory remarks, on the other hand, were not directed to persons who were depressed because of a situation, or because of having sinned.

His remarks therefore have no parallel in earlier writings and are completely original. Support for this conclusion lies in the fact that in his *Synonyma* Isidore referred neither to Cicero nor to Augustine—both of whose works he was thoroughly familiar with. He referred only to Acts 14:21, "For we ought to enter the kindgom of God through much tribulation," and Rom. 8:18, "The sufferings of this world are not comparable to the future glory which shall be revealed in us." A more explicit promise of relief to the person who is depressed without obvious cause is perhaps in John 16:33, "These things I have spoken to you, that in me you may have peace. In the world you shall have distress. But have confidence. I have overcome the world." Scriptural precepts such as these provide an escape from the specific repentance required if a depression is to be considered benign.

Nevertheless, Isidore, like all the other Christian writers on depression, did not distinguish between consciousness of sin and a delusional belief in one's own sinfulness. It was not until the physician Timothy Bright wrote his *Treatise on Melancholie* (22) in 1586 that the distinction was made between true sin and the imagined sin that was a delusional symptom of depression. He wrote: "The afflication of soule through conscience of sinne is quite another thing than melancholy." (It is noteworthy that Bright later gave up the practice of medicine and took holy orders.) There is no way of establishing whether this idea originated with Bright or whether it had been borrowed by him from earlier authors not known to us. (It should be noted that Bright did take from earlier writers without attribution. For example, he clearly did borrow from the writings of the fifth-century physician Caelius Aurelianus, who was the first to refer to the belief that a depressed patient may have the feeling that he is a ceramic pot that might be cracked by ungentle handling, that is, in more modern language, that he might become a crackpot).

With its first-person description of a delusional depression, St. Isidore's work is a medical *landmark*, albeit an unwitting one. However, unless it can be shown to have impressed later medical writers, it cannot be considered a *source*. It is true that symptoms of depression such as Isidore described are common in psychiatric writings of subsequent eras, but it is more likely that they arose out of clinical observations than out of a reading of the *Synonyma*. At the moment no definite link, or chain of links, can be found between the *Synonyma* and modern medical writings in a similar vein.

The question of whether the *Synonyma* might be a source in other fields, such as literature, must also be considered. Isidore's words actually turned up in Hoccleve's *Complaint*, written about 800 years later. Hoccleve was one of Chaucer's disciples, and Chaucer and some of the other disciples are known to have owned and used other works of St. Isidore. However, Hoccleve used only portions of the *Synonyma*, in a work he wrote after 1422, at the age of 53 (23). Much of Hoccleve's literary output up to then and subsequently consisted of complaints about his poverty and the broken promises of his patrons; however he did admit to a very disorderly life. His poem *Complaint* was stimulated by, he said, "a lamentacioun of a wooful man in a book" (23). He omitted to name the book, but the accompanying Latin quotations in some of the extant manuscripts make it plain that the book was Isidore's *Synonyma*. Hoccleve's choice of this work rather than any other to express his own feelings is significant: in the *Complaint* Hoccleve stated that he had just recovered from an attack of madness but that his friends did not believe it. (They may well have been correct.) It is remarkable but not surprising that a recently psychotic person should chose Isidore's words to express his feelings. It is also remarkable, but not surprising, that Hoccleve chose not to use the words of his master, Chaucer, on depression, in the Personnes Tale:

> Thanne cometh the synne of wordly sorwe, is cleped *tristicia*, that sleeth man, as seith seint Paul. For certes, swich sorwe worketh to the deeth of the soule and of the body also; for thereof comth that a man is anoyed of his owene lif. Wherefore swich sorwe shortheth ful ofte of man, er that his time be come by way of kynde.

Hoccleve's *Complaint* describes how the social isolation related to his illness had affected him adversely, but Isidore's words in the unnamed book had given him consolation. Isidore's description of the situation was clearly valid eight centuries later.

It is not known why Hoccleve did not name the book's author. However, it must be remembered that Hoccleve's time was also the time of Wycliffe. Strong anti-Catholic feeling was widespread in England and the unlikely partnership of Wycliffe and John of Gaunt was attempting to destroy the Church's temporal power. Perhaps Hoccleve, a confessed coward, felt that it would be impolitic to name as his inspiration a saint who had done so much to strengthen the power of the Church (in Spain). It is interesting that Hoccleve dedicated the *Complaint* together with some other works to Joanna, daughter of John of Gaunt (23).

It is both disconcerting and tantalizing to find that although Chaucer was interested in depression, his only references to Isidore's writings are to parts of the *Etymologia* (24). Ignoring the *Synonyma* seems to be an established custom among scholars. The remarkable treatise on melancholy written by Klibansky, Panofsky, and Saxl (10) contains ten references to St. Isidore in the text and thirteen more in footnotes, but not one of these refers to Isidore's *Synonyma*.

Isidore's *Synonyma* is an important landmark. It occupies a special place in Christian consolatory literature. It served its consolatory purpose at least once in poetry. Whether or not it was a source in medical history remains to be investigated.

REFERENCES

1. Castro, A. *The structure of Spanish history.* Princeton, N.J.: Princeton University Press, 1954.
2. Lerner, R. E. *The heresy of the free spirit in the later middle ages.* Berkeley: University of California Press, 1972.
3. Rowland, B. *Animals with human faces: A guide to animal symbolism.* Nashville: University of Tennessee Press, ca. 1973.
4. MacKinney, L. *Medical illustrations in medieval manuscripts.* London: Wellcome Historical Medical Library, 1965.
5. Sharpe, W. D. Isidore of Seville: The medical writings. *Transactions of the American Philosophical Society*, Vol. 54, Pt. 2, 1964.
6. Rand, E. K. *Founders of the Middle Ages.* New York: Dover, 1957, pp. 198–200.
7. Endres, J. A. Ueber den Ursprung und die Entwicklung der scholastischen Lehrmethode. *Philosophisches Jahrbuch* 2:52, 1889.
8. Migne, J. P. *Patrologiae Cursus Completus, Sive Biblioteca Universalis . . .* Ser Lat. Vol. 5. Paris: Author, 1862.

9. Mullins, P. J. *The spiritual life according to Saint Isidore of Seville.* Washington, D.C.: Catholic University of America, 1940.

10. Klibansky, R., Panofsky, E., and Saxl, I. *Saturn and melancholy: Studies in the history of natural philosophy, religion, and art.* New York: Basic Books, 1964.

11. Taylor, H. O. *The mediaeval mind: A history of the development of thought and emotion in the middle ages.* Vol. 1. London: Macmillan, 1938.

12. Rigg, A. G. Hoccleve's complaint and Isidore of Seville. *Speculum* 45:564, 1970.

13. Ford, G. B., Jr. *The letters of St. Isidore of Seville.* 2nd rev. ed. Amsterdam: A. M. Hakkert, 1970.

14. de Aldama, J. A. Indicaciones sobre la cronologia de la obras de S. Isidoro. In *Homenaje a S. Isidoro de Sevilla.* Rome: Pontifical Universitatis Gregorianae, 1936.

15. Leclercq, J., Vandenbrouche, R., and Bouyer, L. *The spirituality of the Middle Ages.* London: Burns and Oates, 1968.

16. Leclercq, J. Modern psychology and the interpretation of medieval texts. *Speculum* 48:476, 1973.

17. Adnes, A. Remarques psychobiologiques sur Saint Isidore de Seville. In *Isidoriana.* Leon: Centro de Estudios "San Isidoro," 1961, p. 467.

18. Snyder, S. The left hand of God: Despair in the medieval and Renaissance tradition. *Studies in the Renaissance* 12:18, 1965.

19. Fontaine, J. *Isidore de Séville et la culture classique dans l'Espagne wisigothique.* Paris: Etudes Angustinians, 1959.

20. Cicero. Tusculan Disputations. J. E. Kind, trans. Cambridge, Mass.: Harvard University Press, 1927.

21. *Augustine confessions, with an English translation.* W. Watts, ed. Cambridge, Mass.: Harvard University Press, 1950.

22. Bright, T. *A treatise on melancholie.* London: T. Vautrollier, 1586, pp. 36 ff.

23. Hoccleve, F. J. F., in L. Stephen and S. Lee (Eds.), *Dictionary of National Biography* (Vol. 9). London: Oxford University Press, 1917.

24. Norton-Smith, J. *Geoffrey Chaucer.* Boston: Routledge and Kegan Paul.

Chapter 4

GEORGE CHEYNE
and his English malady

George Cheyne at the height of his fame and perhaps his avoirdupois.

One of the most persistent superstitions of psychology is that there are inborn mental characteristics associated with ethnic groups. These characteristics are held to be immutable, and although sometimes admirable, are usually quite the opposite, or, in some cases, pathologic—for example, the alcoholic Irishman, the stolid Swede, the wily Oriental, the excitable Latin, the cruel Spaniard. These usually derogatory attributions are made by persons of other ethnic groups. The English malady was, however, different. Although it was defined as a pathologic state with pejorative overtones, it was invented, in the eighteenth century, by an Englishman (or rather an anglicized Scot). And George Cheyne (1) was not the first Englishman to maintain that his countrymen were peculiarly susceptible to disease. Gideon Harvey in the previous century had also written about *morbus Anglicus* (2), but he used this term to denote chronic tuberculosis.* Continental physicians were accustomed

---

*"Likewise Grief and study do also by continuation, degenerate into Melancholy Hypochondriack, which afterwards is in a manner a foresaid succeeded by a Consumption. In my other *Morbus Anglicus* you may read several instances of consumption engendered by Love, grief, and study, and therefore I shall omit them here."

Gideon Harvey is today best known for his skepticism as regards medical treatment. His *Art of Curing Disease by Expectation* says (on the first page):

"If Antiquity be capable of conferring Validity, the *Art of Expectation* being contemporary with that of *Physick*, may be termed equally valuable. In many cases they are synonymous, where the Cure is attributed to the Art of Medicine, which in

to calling pulmonary tuberculosis *tabes Anglicus* because of its apparent frequency in England. Harvey, and many others of his era, believed that tuberculosis, as well as every other known disease, was often caused by some extreme and persistent unhealthy state of mind. Hence he held both sides—that tuberculosis might be caused by emotional upset and that it might lead to emotional upset, specifically, severe depression.

Accordingly Harvey's *Morbus Anglicus* might in some cases exhibit manifestations like those emphasized almost a century later by George Cheyne. It was not, however, until George Cheyne had written his *English Malady*, and defined the disease as hypochondriacal depression peculiar to the English, that this English malady received widespread notice in medical writings as a psychiatric disorder.

George Cheyne was born of an old family in Aberdeenshire in northeastern Scotland in 1673 (3, 4), a year after Gideon Harvey published the first edition of his *Morbus Anglicus*. In connection with Cheyne's later illnesses it is interesting that one side of his family manifested a tendency toward obesity; however, there is no information concerning the possibility that Cheyne's nervousness as a schoolboy—a nervousness that "upon the slightest Excesses . . . produced slippery Bowels as well as shaking of his hands . . . . [He had a] Disposition to be easily ruffled on a surprise"—was also familial.

Cheyne's family had included a number of important clergymen, one of whom, Bishop Gilbert Burnet, was to influence his life greatly. Cheyne's younger half-brother later became Vicar of Brigstock, Northampton, and his own son

reality was chiefly performed by the *Art of Expectation*; the Remedies, that were the Tools of the former, being little or no efficacy, and consequently delusory; whereas Time, Delays, and doing nothing, are the principal *media* of the latter. Hence it may easily be apprehended, what is meant by curing Diseases by *Expectation, viz.* the applying of Remedies, that do little hurt, and less good, from which the Patient day by day frustraneously expecting relief, and bennefit, is at last deferred so long, that Nature, and Time have partially, or entirely, cured the Disease, which notwithstanding the Physician by subtlety, cunning, and officiousnes, doth commonly with success insinuate, that the Patient is Debitor for his Life, and recovery, to the Doctor's Skill, Judgment, Method, and Remedies; and in this particular, the wisest of men do become half Fools, by intrusting their Lives, and yielding obedience to most Physicians, of whom, or their Art, they are incapable of judging, by reason of their being unacquainted with the inside of their Persons, and vanities of their Professions."

became Vicar of Weston, near Bath. The strong family interest in religion led Cheyne's parents to prepare him for the Church; he studied at Marischal College, Aberdeen, receiving the then prevailing classical education. However, he became most interested in "abstract sciences," including mathematics. (It is interesting that at that time the study of mathematics was advised to give ballast to an unstable nature.) His strong interest and outstanding competence in mathematics apparently diverted his aim from the clergyman's career to the physician's, but this occurred some years later.

After graduating from Marischal College, Cheyne appears to have become tutor or companion to John Ker, later the first Duke of Roxburgh, Secretary of State for Scotland, Fellow of the Royal Society, and founder of a famous family library. Cheyne's tutoring evidently pertained to religious matters, for when in 1705 he published his *Philosophical Principles of Natural Religion*, he stated that he had written the book to record the discussions the two had had a decade and a half earlier. However, Cheyne's philosophical writings never approached the status of those of some other medical practitioners, such as John Locke and David Hartley.

Some time after 1693, Cheyne decided to study medicine, and although his own writings do not explain in detail this change of mind, the strong urging of Dr. Pitcairne of Edinburgh was evidently a factor. Cheyne was not only interested in mathematics, he came to be regarded by some as one of the greatest mathematicians of his era. (He later wrote several works on integral calculus, then called inverse fluxions.) With this background it is not surprising that a turning point in his career occurred shortly after Archibald Pitcairne returned to Edinburgh in 1693. Pitcairne was a leader of the iatromathematical school of medicine, which taught that all physiological processes, both normal and abnormal, were explicable only as mechanical phenomena and were rigidly determined consequences of the (then known) laws of physics. Descartes, Benini, Borelli, and Sanctorius were its leading theoreticians, and many famous medical teachers adopted the dogma. Pitcairne was not only an outstanding practitioner and teacher of medicine but also an exceptional mathematician, and he used his mathematics in attempting to explain clinical phenomena. Pitcairne's reputation was so great that when the political situation in Scotland forced him into exile, he became professor of medicine at Leyden, maintaining the bond between that medical school and Edinburgh's that lasted until the mid-nineteenth century. He returned to Edinburgh as professor of medicine in 1693. The presence there of a world-famous physician whose basic science was mathematics evidently attracted Cheyne, the devoted mathematician. Pitcairne strongly encouraged Cheyne to study physic.

Cheyne's entry into medicine by way of mathematics resembles the manner in which today many young men, interested and trained in biochemistry, are led into medicine by the mistaken notion that all clinical phenomena can be explained in biochemical terms. Cheyne's devotion to Pitcairne's ideas not only led him into controversies with nonbelievers, but stultified his theoretical discussions of the origin of the English malady, much as some physicians today destroy much of the value of their clinical teaching by insisting on superstitious biochemical or psychological explanations of clinical phenomena. If Cheyne had not written his excellent clinical account of the English malady (1), his name would have been forgotten by all except a few historians. Cheyne's notion that anxious depression—the English malady—was due to generalized stasis caused by abnormal "glewiness, syziness, or viscidity" of the blood sounds like pure nonsense; however, it is no more absurd than are some of the accepted etiological concepts advanced today by biochemical or psychoanalytic dogmatizers.

It must not be concluded that this line of development was the only one open to Cheyne. A striking contrast is afforded by the career of another of Pitcairne's pupils, Hermann Boerhaave, who rejected Pitcairne's iatromathematical dogmas and became one of the greatest clinical teachers of recorded history. Boerhaave, like Sydenham before him, insisted on bedside teaching; his all-encompassing reading and his extensive clinical experience combined to prevent his adopting any of the medical dogmas then current. Although his clinical writings are deficient in original ideas—his works being noteworthy only for their perceptive clinical comments—his clinically trained pupils perpetuated the primacy of Leyden as a clinical center and later established the great clinical tradition of Vienna. His pupils included William Cullen, the great clinician-systematizer; Sir John Pringle, the founder of military medicine; Anton de Haen, who introduced the clinical thermometer; Gerhard van Swieten, the founder of the Vienna School; Hieronymus Gaub, the integrator of physiology with medicine; and even Albrecht von Haller, master physiologist and medical historian. Cheyne left no such legacy.

In 1701, some time after finishing his medical studies, Cheyne published anonymously a book on fevers; later editions appeared under his own name. True to the iatromathematical tradition, it was more mathematical than clinical and today is only of historical interest. However, it impressed some members of the Royal Society—probably including his relative Bishop Burnet—who invited him to come to London. Before leaving Edinburgh, he was granted (on September 8, 1701) the degree of doctor *in medicinae gratis* because, according to the records of the college, "He's not only our owne countryman, and at present not rich, but is recommended by the ablest and most learned Physicians in Edinburgh as one of the best mathematicians in Europe; and for his skill in medicine he hath given a sufficient indication of that by his learned Tractat *De Febribus*, which hath made him famous abroad as well as at home; and he being just now goeing to England upon invitation of some of the members of the Royal Society."

He began to practice in London shortly afterward. The London practitioner's life at that time was an interesting mixture of study and hard work combined with tavern diversion. Dr. Viets's account (4) portrays this vividly. One of Cheyne's friends, his fellow physician Richard Mead, is said to have started up the ladder of professional fame—he ultimately became physician to King George I—because of this life. Mead had spent one evening, as was customary for beginners in practice, in steady drinking. When a noblewoman living nearby became ill, and could not get word to her regular physician, her servant went to a tavern frequented by young practitioners, where he found Mead, who despite his inebriation was called to attend the duchess. As Mead entered her chamber, he tripped over a rug and exclaimed "Drunk again!" The duchess, under the impression that he was referring to her, begged him not to tell her husband. According to one account, Mead's discretion evoked the gratitude of the lady, and she repaid him by praising his medical knowledge to her many rich and powerful friends. He thus gained many opportunities to distinguish himself in the richest and most powerful social group in the country.

As Cheyne himself wrote in *The English Malady* (1), on coming to London, he changed his whole manner of living, becoming the intimate of "bottle-companions, the younger gentry, and free-livers." His ability to eat and drink lustily, together with his cheerful nature and lively imagination, made him their favorite. However, he "grew daily in bulk" and "grew excessively fat, short-breathed, lethargic, and listless." In short, he developed cor pulmonale owing to extreme obesity. (This is now called the Pickwickian syndrome, after the Fat Boy in the *Pickwick Papers*.) Cheyne developed a febrile illness of some type, and this left him dull, depressed, and subject to dizzy attacks. He could scarcely get about, and his "holiday friends" soon deserted him, dropping off "like autumnal leaves." His feelings of despondency, anxiety, and guilt worsened. At this point, when he was forty-two years old, he took the advice of physician friends to limit himself to a diet of milk and a few vegetables. He rode horseback every day, spending the summers in Bath and winters in London, in both of which he practiced his profession; he gradually changed his diet, living on light and tender animal foods instead of milk and vegetables. His long idleness had turned his mind to philosophy once more, and, in 1715, he wrote the second part of his *Philosophical Principles of Religions.*

A few years later his brief work on gout, essentially a work in praise of the waters of Bath, appeared. At this time his practice had come to include many of the notable persons of the period; Samuel Johnson, John Wesley, Beau Nash, David Hume, Alexander Pope, Samuel Richardson were among them. He corresponded with most of them and also with many other prominent persons of London and Bath. Cheyne's relations with Samuel Richardson are particularly interesting, not only because of their nature and duration but because the letters between the two men have been preserved (5). Richardson, a sufferer from chronic anxiety and its associated somatic symptoms, received much medical advice in these letters. In addition, Cheyne gave Richardson unsolicited advice on how to make his novels more interesting. In his letter of August 24, 1841, Cheyne wrote "I think you are right to begin with the least promising Parts and rise gradually on your Reader. . . . Readers love Rapidity in Narrations and quick Returns. Keep them from dosing [*sic*]." For his part, Richardson gave Cheyne professional advice, and despite Cheyne's denunciations of Richardson's brother-in-law, Leake the printer, Richardson patiently guided Cheyne's writings to ultimate publication.

Cheyne's recovery led him to become caught up in his professional and social lives once more, and soon he began to neglect the thin diet that had helped him so greatly. He began to gain weight again, and after a dozen years he weighed about 450 pounds. The slightest exertion caused extreme dyspnoea, cyanosis, and dizziness; he could not walk a hundred steps on the flat without resting. He became extremely lethargic again. A severe febrile illness and then a violent attack of erysipelas followed. Cheyne became so markedly disabled that he sought the aid of a half-dozen physicians, including Mead, in December 1725. Once more he went on his former diet of milk and vegetables, and by 1732 was again completely well. He continued to take the diet for the rest of his life. His book *An Essay of Health and Long Life* (6) was published in 1724, having been written at a time when his health was failing. *The English Malady* was published in 1733, when he was well again, and firmly convinced that his life depended on his milk and vegetable diet. As the preface of the former work makes clear, he was depressed—suffering from "fluctuation and indocility, scrupulosity, horror, and despair." The book made some references to the disorder that was treated systematically in *The English Malady*, but its main content bore on the regimen he favored.

The reason for making milk the main item of diet is not evident. Cheyne apparently admired milk-drinkers, and quoted with approval Homer's words on the Scythians (although it was mare's milk that they drank): "Simple in manners, poor, living on milk, the most honourable of men." Actually, physicians have believed in the virtues of milk for centuries, and as recently as the first part of this century a milk diet (Karrell diet) was popular in treating congestive failure. Today the drinking of large amounts of milk is taken by some as evidence of an unresolved Oedipus complex.

An Essay of Health and Long Life brought him popular renown and apparently earned him an honorary fellowship in the College of Physicians of Edinburgh in 1724. The milk diet he recommended was widely adopted for the treatment of any illness alleged to have a psychological origin. For example, as Aileen Ward (7) notes in her *John Keats*, pulmonary tuberculosis was considered a psychosomatic disorder and, naturally, was treated by the customary milk and vegetable diet. However, Cheyne's regimen also aroused opposition and ridicule among some physicians and others. Since, in recommending it, he derogated luxury and gluttony, he was accused of everything from mere silliness to wanting to destroy the social order. He replied to some of his critics and ignored others.

One of the more amiable exchanges occurred when a Dr. Wright wrote:

> Tell me from whom, fat-headed Scot,
> Thou didst thy system learn;
> From Hippocrate thou hast it not,
> Nor Celsus, nor Pitcairne.
>
> Suppose we own that *milk* is good,
> And say the same of *grass*;
> The one for *babes* is only food,
> The other for an *ass*.
>
> Doctor! one new prescription try,
> (A friend's advice forgive;)
> Eat grass, reduce thyself, and *die*;
> Thy *patients* then may live.

To this Cheyne replied:

> My "system," Doctor is my own,
> No tutor I pretend:
> *My* blunders hurt myself alone,
> But *yours* your dearest friend.

Were *you* to milk and straw confined,
Thrice happy might you be;
Perhaps you might regain your mind,
And from your wit get free.

I cannot your "prescription try,"
But heartily "forgive";
Tis nat'ral you should bid *me* "die,"
That you yourself may "live."

Boswell wrote (in his *Life of Johnson*), "He [Johnson] recommended Dr. Cheyne's books. I said I thought Cheyne had been reckoned whimsical, 'So he was,' said he, 'in some things; but there is no end of objections. There are few books to which some objection or other may not be made.' He added, 'I would not have you read any thing else of Cheyne, but his book on *Health*, and his *English Malady*!' " It is worthy of note that Samuel Johnson was not only a great hypochondriac but he also suffered from cor pulmonale secondary to pulmonary emphysema. Fielding, in his *Tom Jones*, also praised Cheyne's ideas, and John Wesley, in his writings on health (8), copied them. (Wesley's book was highly popular in both Great Britain and North America.)

After Cheyne published his *English Malady*, he reworked the contents of some of his earlier books and published them in 1739 in *An Essay on Regimen* (9). Although he considered it the best book he had ever written, it did not have as favorable a reception as did his previous writings. However, he continued to practice and lead a very active social life until about ten days before his death. The details of his last illness are not known, and in fact his death was not expected. He did not ask for professional help until the day before his death, when he called in, quite appropriately, the physician-philosopher David Hartley (whose *Observations on Man* marked the beginning of the associationist theory in modern psychology). Mrs. Cheyne's brother, Dr. Middleton, was also in attendance. Cheyne was buried in Weston near Bath where other members of his family lay.

As regards *The English Malady* itself, three questions require consideration:

1. Why did he write the book despite the fact that, as he put it, "I never wrote a book in my Life but I had a fit of illness after"?

2. Why did he call it *The English Malady*?

3. What influence did the book have on clinical concepts and practice?

With respect to the first, it is clear that *The English Malady* was largely stimulated by self-observation. A question regarding the origin of his symptoms therefore arises. Anxiety and depression commonly occur in patients with cor pulmonale, and hence it is possible that his anxious depression might have been due solely to this disease. Cheyne makes it clear that his psychological symptoms improved at the same time as his symptoms of cor pulmonale; hence the cardiovascular disease might well have caused the psychiatric disorder. On the other hand, his nervousness long antedated his cor pulmonale. Moreover, although he declared himself cured of his depression after recovering from his illness, his own writings prove otherwise. For example, before he became ill at the age of forty-two, he was cheerful, gay, and witty. His appearance and behavior were recorded in *McMichael's Gold-Headed Cane* (second edition, 1828). The occasion was the illness of his relative, Bishop Burnet, and Cheyne had called Hans Sloane and Richard Mead as consultants. The actual observer responsible for this account is not known, but the description sounds accurate:

On the other side was Dr. Cheyne, a Scotsman, with an immense broad back, taking snuff incessantly out of a ponderous gold box, and thus ever and anon displaying to view his fat knuckles: a perfect Falstaff, for he was not only a good portly man and a corpulent, but was almost as witty as the knight himself, and his humour being brightened by his northern brogue, he was exceedingly mirthful. Indeed he was the most excellent banterer of his time, a faculty he was often called upon to exercise, to repel the lampoons which were made by others upon his extraordinary appearance.

However, after his ostensible recovery from his illness, his personality was entirely different. His writings reveal the humorlessness and lugubrious piety that indicate persistence of depression. The surviving writings include his letters to the Countess of Huntingdon (10)—herself a person of formidable piety—and to Samuel Richardson (5). For example, his letter to Richardson advising him what to put in his novels reveals Cheyne's changed character more accurately than do his autobiographical writings, because the latter discussed almost exclusively the events of his life and his feelings during his illnesses. Cheyne told Richardson to include as interesting incidents

either Distresses naturally overcome or good Fortune unexpectedly happening. . . . For example a broken Leg, a disjointed limb, a dangerous Fever, happening to a Husband and then the tender Care, Vigilance, and active Nursing of a loving Wife, and then she would have an opportunity to insinuate all the noble and beautiful Sentiments to a rakish or unconverted infidel. . . . I would pick out all the events of Conjunct lives and insinuate proper Behaviour under them. The Death of a favourite Child, a sudden Conflagration of one's own or his Neighbour's favourite Seat, an Epidemical Distemper, a severe Winter, a Famine, etc. . . .

Richardson wrote in a letter to Stephen Duck (11): "An excellent Physician was so good as to give me a Plan to break Legs and Arms and to fire Mansions to create Distresses." Cheyne went on, "You ought to avoid Fondling and Gallantry, tender Expressions not becoming the Character of Wisdom, Piety, and conjugal Chastity. . . . Clasping, kissing, stroking, hugging are but Approaches to those others and are really dangerous to be proposed to or read by young Persons of either Sex" (5).

Cheyne evidently believed that man is vile, whereas woman might not be. In the same letter he says, "I would make my Heroine convert my hero, for Religion and Seriousness is more the character of the Women than the Men. The first are more gentle, docile, and meek in the Main, and the latter more sturdy, rough, and *esprits Forts*." However, further along in the same letter he says, "I know no difference between the Sexes but in their Configuration." Cheyne's piety gained him many readers, and his biography, published in 1846, was one of a series of "the lives of physicians who have been eminent for their piety" (3). The editor stated that he would "be deeply pained, if any person of piety and good sense shall consider, either that he has inserted in his list any name but those of Physicians really fearing *God* and loving Christ, or that he has published any life written in a low or unchristian spirit." The almost voluptuous delight that Cheyne took in revealing his sufferings is the mark of the neurotic depressive. The best conclusion is that his psychiatric disorder was not caused by his cor pulmonale, although clearly it was aggravated by it. Hence we may conclude that Cheyne really had the English malady, an apparently idiopathic anxious depression.

The question concerning his reason for calling the disorder the English malady can be answered more positively. Interest in this disorder began centuries earlier, as discussions of anxiety and depression in lay writings going back many years attest. The two symptoms were commonly discussed together. In 1745, Cheyne's contemporary, Foster (12), wrote in *A Treatise on the Causes of Most Diseases Incident to Human Bodies*: "Melancholy madness is commonly no more than hypochondriacal affection aggravated." However, the union of the two was an ancient one. One book, Burton's *Anatomy of Melancholy* (13), first published in 1621, came to be one of the most famous books ever written in the English language, and it too united the two symptoms, as had authors of the previous thousand years and more.

As regards anxiety, the modern era began with Locke (14), who naturally took a philosophical view of it, as his *Essay Concerning Human Understanding* indicates. He wrote:

> What is it that determines the will in regard to our actions? And that, upon second thoughts, I am apt to imagine is not, as is generally supposed, the greater good in view, but some (and for the most part the most pressing) uneasiness a man is at present.... All pain of the body, of what sort soever, and disquiet of the mind, is uneasiness.... The greatest present uneasiness is the spur of action that is constantly felt, and for the most part, determines the will in its choice of the next action.

From the English psychiatric writings of the late seventeenth to the mid-nineteenth centuries, it is evident that interest in anxiety and depression was almost a tradition. Cheyne's stated reason for calling his work *The English Malady* was that it was "a reproach universally thrown on this Island by foreigners and all our neighbours on the Continent, by whom nervous distempers, spleen, vapours, and lowness of spirits, are in derision called *The English Malady*." Here it seems as though the foreigners had given the syndrome its name. Yet in his preface Cheyne wrote:

> If a Phthisis is justly called by Foreigners "Tabes Anglica," or the "English" Consumption, because it is most predominant, and in a manner peculiar to this Country; I am well assured there is no less Reason to give to the Distemper I have chosen for the Subject of this Treatise, the Appellation of the "English" Spleen; since it has here gained such a universal and tyrannical Dominion over both Sexes, as incomparably exceeds its Power in other Nations: for though in foreign Climates, especially those nearer the Sun, Disorders of Mind, Lunacy, and disturbed Imagination, are very frequent; yet the English Spleen, as I have now named it, and as I have described it in the following Pages, is comparatively but seldom found among the Inhabitants of other Countries.

There is no doubt that Cheyne's views were widely accepted, but not necessarily in the form in which he had expressed them. On the Continent, Lorry (15) in 1765 and de Sauvages (16) in 1772 discussed the English malady in general terms, but Pinel (17) in 1806 was much more specific—he regarded the malady as a syndrome of self-destruction when he accepted and referred approvingly to the earlier words of Montesquieu:

> The English frequently destroy themselves without any apparent cause to determine them to such an act, and even in the midst of prosperity. Among the Romans suicide was the effect of education; it depended upon the customs and manner of thinking: with the English it is the effect of disease, and depending upon the physical condition of the system.

(Whoever had originally owned my copy of Pinel's work had written in an old script, "There was no doubt of this truth.") One of Pinel's followers, Jacquelin-Dubuisson (18), had even more to say:

> The spleen, English malady, or consumption, is a type of melancholy with a tendency toward suicide. There are not many disappointments, adversities, or violent passions among the causes of that disease. On the contrary, those who are afflicted, free from suffering and torment, have

*A French lithograph by an unknown early eighteenth-century artist
indicative of what the French thought of the English.*

been raised in opulence, they have been endowed with excess and satiated
in all types of pleasures that have weakened their sensibilities: they no
longer experience those feelings of affection, of tenderness and of interest
that bind us to our families, that tie us to our friends, that make us love
our country as the cradle of our birth. In short, they become incapable of
experiencing any emotion, of having any desire or regret, of conceiving of
any hope or uncertainty. That state of inertia and enfeeblement of the
sensitive and moral faculties throws these patients into emaciation,
marasmus, and consumption, renders their existence a burden, and
encourages them to free themselves by a fatal attempt.

This sickness is most common in England, where it seems to
have been endemic for a long time, since Dr. Cheyne says, in the
preface of his book, printed in 1733, that he had been in haste
to publish his treatise on the English malady because of the
constantly increasing number of suicides:

The frequency of the spleen, in England, is attributable to the moist
and foggy state of the atmosphere, to the abuse by the inhabitants of
spirituous drinks, as well as the mental turmoil induced in them by the
austerities of some religious sects, and the hazardous chances of maritime

commerce. Those who are afflicted are commonly the rich capitalists who abuse, instead of wisely using, the variable favors of fortune, and who ignore the so useful art of making the satisfaction of pure happinesses and lasting pleasures serve them properly. One also finds this illness in Scotland, among the inhabitants of the mountain gorges, where the air is moist, foggy and stagnant, and where the food is coarse and unhealthy. . . .

Esquirol (19), a Belgian, was equally severe in his comments:

In England, where we find united all the caprices, as well as the excesses, of civilization, insanity is more frequent than anywhere else. Unsuitable marriages; those contracted by parents, and above all, alliances formed with families where there is an hereditary predisposition to insanity, the hazards of remote speculations, the indolence of the rich, and the habitual use of alcoholic drinks, are the causes which multiply insanity in England.

Greisinger (20), a German, limited his comments to certain English spinsters:

The number of cases of insanity occurring amongst young female teachers and governesses is, at all events in England, very great: Bedlam received in 10 years (1846-55) 110 such young women. Here adverse fortune, want of rest, excessive mental exertion, and a disagreeable life may be the chief causes.

Baron von Feuchtersleben, dean of the Medical School of Vienna and councilor to the Emperor Francis Joseph, provided a wordly but sensible comment (21). After noting that Great Britain was a "country where originality has been carried even to eccentricity," he said:

The observation that national peculiarities are reflected in concrete cases of insanity, through certainly correct in itself (for even with a broken leg the genuine Frenchman will behave differently from the genuine Englishman), would lead to uselsss trifling if we were to pursue it further.

However, it was English physicians who had the most to say and who specifically ascribed interest in the syndrome to George Cheyne's writings. Arnold (22), sixty-five years after Cheyne, was doubtful. He wrote:

Whether Insanity Prevails More In England Than In Other Countries

Insanity, especially of the melancholy kind, has been commonly supposed to prevail so much more in this island than in any other part of Europe, that it has acquired among foreigners the denomination of the English Disease. How justly, might be difficult to determine. There is, I believe, some foundation for the supposition; though, perhaps much less than is generally imagined.

Trotter (23), in 1807, was much more positive about the validity of the syndrome:

Dr. Cheyne, who wrote about the year 1733, in his work entitled the "English Malady," makes nervous disorders almost one third of the complaints of people of condition in England: from which we are led to believe, they were then little known among the inferior orders. But from causes, to be hereafter investigated, we shall find, that nervous ailments are no longer confined to the better ranks in life, but rapidly extending to the poorer classes. In this neighbourhood, as far as I am able to judge from my own experience, they are by no means limited to the rich: and it affords a

George Cruikshank's representation of his own miseries.

melancholy picture of the health of the community, to observe this proportion so very large. It is probable the other countries of Europe do not exhibit such general examples of these diseases; as many of their causes are to be traced to the peculiar situation of Britain; its insular varieties of climate and atmosphere; its political institutions and free government; and above everything, its vast wealth, so diffused among all ranks of people.

A few years later Cox (24) wrote:

Most of our formidable maladies are rare, but insanity is unfortunately not only frequent but said to be peculiarly endemical to England; nor are we left to conjecture the causes. Early dissipation, unrestrained licentiousness, habitual luxury, inordinate taste for speculation, defective systems of education, laxity of morals; but more especially, promiscuous intermarriages, where one or both of the parties have hereditary claims to alienation of mind, are sufficient to explain the lamentable fact. Where few or none of these causes exist, madness is a rare occurrence or wholly unknown.

Burrows' somewhat bitter remarks (25) also ascribed the common use of the term "English" malady to Cheyne's writings:

Foreigners of all countries pronounce insanity as the opprobrium of England. This not an obsolete prejudice, but one that is current; and has recently been openly promulgated, even in our very halls. Dr. Spurzhein remarks, that it is certain there are more insane people in Great Britain and Ireland than elsewhere, and most in England. This, however, is obviously an imported, not a practical, observation. As Dr. Spurzheim had no better opportunity than others of ascertaining the number of insane persons in this kingdom, how then was it possible that he could form any estimate of the comparative prevalence of the malady? Or why announce it to be an endemic?

Dr. Lorry says, that melancholy is a vice born with, and endemical in, the English; and again, that they fall into it without any obvious cause; and that, upon a change of atmosphere, it will entirely vanish, as if by a miracle. Others have pronounced a similar judgement. But while Lorry stigmatizes the English as prone to insanity, and designates it morbus Anglicus, he compliments the natives by admitting that it frequently originates in their attachment to scientific pursuits. . . .

Why the English have been supposed to be more obnoxious to mental maladies than other people, I have never, though sedulously inquiring, been able to discover. May not this obloquy have originated in Dr. G. Cheyne's popular treatise, entitled "The English Malady"? There is scarcely a foreign writer who does not quote his authority for imputing to the natives of this island an extraordinary predisposition to melancholy; and particularly to a species of hypochondriacism, to which Dr. Cheyne gave the generic term "Spleen"; and which foreign nosologists have introduced into their systems, and classed by this vernacular appellation.

Having once imbibed an opinion, that the English were peculiarly prone to insanity, it was no violent assumption to infer, that they must consequently be most devoted to the practice of suicide. Accordingly, we find divines, philosphers, poets, and authors of all kinds, adopting it as an historic fact; and attaching this crime as innate in the British character. Even the celebrated Montesquieu has condescended to become a vehicle of this calumny.

Feeling as a Briton, jealous of the moral, as well as of the religious principles of my countrymen, I have before endeavoured to repel this charge.

Reid's words (26) were more dramatic:

The subject of lunacy and of lunatic asylums is one of peculiar interest to the British practitioner. By its visible and rapid extension, insanity renders itself every day more deserving of the title of the English malady. Madness strides like a colossus over this island.

Actually the early prevalence of the idea that the English were considered particularly susceptible to mental and emotional disorders is exemplified by these lines from Hamlet (Act V, Scene 1):

Hamlet: Ay, marry, why was he sent into England?
Clown: Why, because he was mad. He shall recover his wits there; or, if he do not, 'tis no great matter there.
Hamlet: Why?
Clown: 'Twill not be seen in him there. There the men are as mad as he.*

*Many writers stated that the English were particularly susceptible to mental disease. This susceptibility seems to have spread somewhat. After Jonathan Swift established St. Patrick's Hospital for the Insane in Dublin, he wrote a few satirical couplets to celebrate the event. These stated:

He gave what little wealth he had
To build a house for fools and mad;
And show'd by one satiric touch,
No nation needed it so much.

from Williams, H., ed. The Poems of Jonathan Swift. Vol. 2. Oxford: Clarendon Press, 1935, p. 751.

The significance of Cheyne's book lies in several areas. For one thing, the work early participated in, and to a great extent later stimulated, the growth of interest in anxiety and depression that was developing in eighteenth-century medicine in Great Britain. The book was also widely read in lay circles. The work itself consists of parts of unequal interest and significance. The section on etiology presents the basic mechanisms in iatromathematical terms, terms of pure nonsense. However, the precipitating causes are more familiar today, if no more capable of being validated. Cheyne believed that aside from certain peculiarities of the English climate, the main causes were related to luxury: "the richness and heaviness of our food, the wealth and abundance of the inhabitants (from their universal trade), the inactivity and sedentary occupation of the better sort (amongst whom this evil mostly rages), and the humour of living in great populous and consequently unhealthy towns." He described the occurrence of anxious and depressive disorders as "scarce known to our ancestors and never rising to such fatal heights, nor affecting such numbers in any known nation. These disorders being computed to make almost one-third of the complaints of the people of condition in England." The idea that luxury was the cause was repeated in other statements:

Assemblies, Musick Meetings, Plays, Cards, and Dice, are the only Amusements, or perhaps business followed by such persons as live in the manner mentioned [i.e., in idle luxury]. . . . And to convey them with the least Pain and Uneasiness possible from motion, or slavish Labour, to these still and bewitching Employments: Coaches are improved with Springs, Horses are taught to pace and amble, Chairmen to wiggle and swim along.

The part about carriage springs evidently made a strong impression, for Reid repeated it in 1823 in his *Essays on Hypochondriasis and Other Nervous Affections* (26). Yet we note that this same author's treatise on consumption (27) is a straightforward clinical account of the disease, with no attempt to ascribe it to purported psychologic characteristics of the English people. Although Reid noted the frequency of pulmonary tuberculosis in England, he did not call it the *English Malady*.

The main value of Cheyne's *The English Malady* lies not in

its absurd or quaint notions of etiology but in its eloquent and perceptive clinical descriptions of the "apprehension and re-morse . . . a perceptual anxiety and inquietude . . . a melancholy fright and panick, where my reason was of no use to me." The evolution and regression, the fluctuation and changing character of symptoms of the disorder, were all described in words recognizable not only to physicians but to their patients who had the disorder. By 1821, Graham, not a psychiatrist but a stomach specialist, was using language that many today believe was invented during what is called our Age of Anxiety. He wrote (28):

Individual wealth has accumulated in this Kingdom within the last thirty or forty years beyond all precedent, the acquisition of which has been attended (as the history of the world proves it ever has been, and ever will be) with unusual anxiety, and diminished bodily exercise of a salubrious kind. . . . It must not be forgotten, that independently of the anxiety attending an eager pursuit of business, the uniform result of success is a greater style of living, which invariably brings with it an increase of care, and multiplies the sources not of enjoyment, but of disquietude.

Cheyne's book is also important for its emphasis on the close relations between these psychological symptoms and a wide variety of bodily complaints. A century and a half later Hecker began to talk of somatic symptoms as "anxiety equiva-lents," and Freud later claimed this concept as his own. Cheyne's writing clearly foreshadowed this.

Cheyne's attempt to find a unitary explanation of the disorder failed because he was committed to iatromathematical superstitions. Not until the second half of the eighteenth century did the increasing information about the sympathetic nervous system suggest a rational mechanism for the symptoms of the English malady. The way in which this information was used was epitomized by Trotter (23) when he wrote: "There is not a muscle or organ of the body that receives a single tendril of the sympathetic nerve without partaking more or less in these diseased feelings." The modern (nonpsychodynamic) concept of neurotic disorders was thus born.

The second half of the eighteenth century saw an unprec-edented amount of discussion of anxiety and melancholy as medical, rather than moral, phenomena, and Cheyne's extensive writings in this field were highly influential in this development. Equally important was the effect of Cheyne's work in changing ideas about basic aspects of anxiety. Johannes Wier, in *On the Delusions of Demons* (29), moved delusions, and Thomas Willis, in *Two Discourses Concerning the Soul of Brutes* (30), moved hallucinations from the realm of the moral to the realm of the medical. And a host of continental medical writers did the same for depressions; similarly Cheyne—albeit inadvertently—made English physicians aware of the fact that anxiety was to be regarded as a medical rather than a moral disorder. Even though Cheyne considered it to be caused by violations of moral tenets, the fact that a variety of somatic complaints accompanied it and that physical treatment might ameliorate the disorder made physicians regard it in a different light.

Thus Cheyne was an important force in the development of basic concepts of twentieth-century psychiatry, although his notion that there was a specific disease that only the English had was abandoned as the nineteenth century wore on. However the notion was reborn, peculiarly; it became Beard's "American nervousness" (31):

While modern nervousness is not peculiar to America, yet there are special expressions of this nervousness that are found here only; and the relative quantity of nervousness and of nervous diseases that spring out of nervousness, are far greater here than in any other nation in history, and it has a special quality. . . . The nervousness of America is extending over Europe, which, in certain countries, at least, is becoming rapidly Americanized.

Beard, however, ascribed the illness to repressed emotions: "The cause of the increase of nervous diseases is that the conventionalities of society require the emotions to be repressed." This notion did not originate with Beard but was expressed in one way or another in English and Continental writing of the mid-nineteenth century.

Beard's discussion can only be considered trivial as regards Cheyne. Except for the name of the syndrome, he clearly got little from Cheyne. Cheyne's influence was felt more strongly on the Continent, where *angst* became the key that unlocked the secrets of mental and emotional disorders for a number of influential psychiatrists.

REFERENCES

1. Cheyne, G. *The English malady: or a treatise of nervous diseases of all kinds.* London: G. Strahan, 1733.
2. Harvey, G. *Morbus Anglicus, or a theoretick and practical discourse of consumptions and hypochondriack melancholy.* London: W. Thackeray, ca. 1780, p. 55.
3. Greenhill, W. A. *Life of George Cheyne, M.D.* Oxford: J. II. Parker; London: John Churchill; 1846.
4. Viets, H. R. The Fielding H. Garrison Lecture, George Cheyne (1673–1743). *Bulletin of the History of Medicine* 23:435, 1949.
5. Mullett, C. F. *The letters of Dr. George Cheyne to Samuel Richardson (1713–1743).* Columbia, Mo.: University of Missouri, 1943.
6. Cheyne, G. *An essay of health and long life.* London: G. Strahan, 1724.
7. Ward, A. *John Keats: The making of a poet.* New York: Viking Press, 1963.
8. Wesley, J. *Rev. John Wesley's valuable primitive remedies, or an easy and natural method of curing most diseases.* Chicago: O. W. Gordon, 1880.
9. Cheyne, G. *An essay of regimen.* London: C. Rivington, 1740.
10. Mullett, C. F. *The letters of George Cheyne to the Countess of Huntingdon.* San Marino, Calif.: Huntington Library, 1940.
11. Carroll, J. *Selected letters of Samuel Richardson.* Oxford, England: Clarendon Press, 1964.
12. Forster, W. *A treatise on the causes of most diseases incident to human bodies, and the cure of them.* Leeds, England: J. Lester, 1745.
13. Burton, R. *The anatomy of melancholy . . . A new edition corrected and enriched by translation of the numerous classical extracts.* Boston: Dana Estes, n.d.
14. Locke, J. *An essay concerning human understanding.* 19th ed. London: T. Longmans, 1793.
15. Lorry, A. C. *De melancholia et morbis melancholicis.* Lutetiae Parisiorum: G. Cavelier, 1765, p. 48.
16. De Sauvages. B. *Nosologie méthodique ou distribution des maladies en classes, en genies et en species, suivant l'esprit de Sydenham et la méthode des botanistes.* M. Gouvion, trans. Lyon: J.-M. Bruyset, 1772.
17. Pinel, P. *A treatise on insanity.* D. D. Davis, trans. Sheffield: W. Todd, 1806, p. 146.
18. Jacquelin-Dubuisson, J. R. *Des vesanies, ou maladies mentales.* Paris: Chez Pasteur, 1816, p. 116.

19. Esquirol, E. *Mental maladies: A treatise on insanity.* E. K. Hunt, trans. Philadelphia: Lea and Blanchard, 1845.

20. Greisinger, W. *Mental pathology.* Trans. from the 2nd German ed. by C. Lockhart Robertson and J. Rutherford. London: New Sydenham Society, 1867, p. 200.

21. Von Feuchtersleben, E. *The principles of medical psychology.* H. E. Lloyd, trans. London: Sydenham Society, 1847, p. 254.

22. Arnold, T. *Observations on the nature, kinds, causes, and prevention of insanity, lunacy, or madness.* Vol. 1. Leicester: G. Robinson; London: T. Cadell; 1782, p. 15.

23. Trotter, T. *A view of the nervous temperament.* London: Longman, Hurst, Rees, and Orme, 1807.

24. Cox, J. M. *Practical observations in insanity.* Philadelphia: T. Dobson, 1811.

25. Burrows, G. M. *An inquiry into certain errors relative to insanity.* London: T. and G. Underwood, 1820, p. 83.

26. Reid, J. *Essays on hypochondriasis and other nervous affections.* London: Longman, Hurst, Rees, Orme, and Brown, 1823, p. 310.

27. Reid, J. *A treatise on the origin, progress, prevention, and treatment of consumption.* London: R. Phillips, 1806.

28. Graham, T. J. *A treatise on indigestion.* Philadelphia: Key and Mielke, 1831.

29. Wier, J. *Histoires, disputes et discours des illusions et impostures des diables, des magiciens infames, sorciers et empoisonneurs.* Paris: Delahayeet Legrosnier, 1885.

30. Willis, T. *Two discourses concerning the soul of brutes which is that of the vital and sensitive of man.* S. Pordage, trans. London: T. Dring, 1683.

31. Beard, G. M. *American nervousness.* New York: G. P. Putnam & Sons, 1881, p. 13.

Chapter 5

ACEDIA
*its evolution from deadly sin
to psychiatric syndrome*

*Part of a painting c. 1475, Hieronymous Bosch, picturing the
seven deadly sins, of which acedia was one. Philip II of Spain
kept this painting in his bedroom.*

Iohannes Cassianus, more commonly known as John Cassian, wrote his treatise *De Institutis Coenobiorum et de Octo Principalium Vitiorum Remediis, Libri XII* around the beginning of the fifth century A.D. (1). This work is important because it introduced certain Eastern ideas into Western thought. Some of these ideas are of considerable psychiatric interest.

Cassian first studied with St. Jerome in the East, and then during the ten years from 390 to 400 he toured the parts of Egypt that were inhabited by anchorites and cenobites. After this he spent many years studying in Constantinople under St. John Chrysostom and other Eastern scholars. In 415 he founded his own monastery at Marseilles. The first four volumes of his treatise comprise a detailed account of the organization of a monastery; the last eight discuss the principal sins and their cure. In Cassian's work the deadly sins number eight; this number was subsequently reduced to seven by Pope Gregory the Great. However, some Carolingian and later theologians continued to list eight, although others listed only seven. Neither the number nor the identity of the cardinal sins became fixed until many centuries after Cassian (2).

Cassian discussed the sins largely in relation to the behavior of monks. He apparently derived many of his ideas from earlier comments on monastic life by Evagrius Ponticus, who in the fourth century A.D. had constructed a list of eight chief "evil thoughts" that afflicted monks. Cassian introduced the eight deadly sins to the Latin West; these sins, in decreasing order of deadliness, were, according to Cassian: (1) pride, (2) vanity, (3) acedia—later called accidia, (4) depression or pessimism, (5) anger, (6) avarice, (7) fornication, and (8) gluttony. Most of these are familiar to modern readers, but one of them, acedia, is not. The word had different meanings to different writers. Thus Evagrius Ponticus used it to denote the boredom in a monk that made him fall asleep in his cell or else desert his religious profession altogether.* However, his writings apparently had little direct influence on later Western scholars. On the other hand, Cassian defined acedia as "taedium sive anxietas cordis." This phrase may be translated as "disgust or boredom, which can be otherwise called inquietude or perturbation of the heart or anxiety." (Referring anxiety to the heart was common in the ancient East; it is to be found in the Old Testament and in Greek writings.) In fact, Cassian specifically used the word *inquietudo* to describe acedia. The implication of a relation between anxiety and boredom is worth discussing, particularly since anxiety itself is currently accorded excessive importance. In addition, tedium also has a connotation of depression; a relation between anxiety and depression has been recognized for years.

Before acedia itself is discussed, one other matter must be considered. According to Cassian, feelings of anger, acedia, and depression were deadly sins; however, today they are regarded as psychiatric symptoms. The same might be said somewhat less emphatically about others of the deadly sins. It must be

---

*Several Fathers of the Church have warned that acedia, or spiritual sloth in cloistered men, may be caused by the attack of the Noonday Demon. (See Arbesmann, R. "The 'Daemonium Meridianum' and Greek and Latin Patristic Exegesis." *Traditio* 14:17-31, 1958.) On the other hand, this Demon was also held responsible for the seduction of fair ladies (see Friedman, J. B. "Euridice, Heurodis, and the Noon-Day Demon." *Speculum* 41:22-29, 1966).

The idea that the Noonday Demon, the Daemonium Meridianum, was merely a roguish sprit who delighted in attacking people at midday when they felt languid, leading men to lose their ambition and women their virtue, is not entirely accurate. To Thomas More the Noonday Demon was the one who also persuaded the susceptible to seek persecution and thereby be forced to forswear their Christianity. (See More, T. *Utopia and A Dialogue of Comfort Against Tribulation.* L. Miles, ed. Bloomington: Indiana University Press, 1965, p. 237.) More's usage was evidently an extension of the concept of "the devil in midday," presented in Ps. 9:6.

remembered in this connection that Cassian studied in the East for about twenty-five years, and Eastern ideas certainly had a great influence on his own thinking. Primitive Eastern religions, as with those in some other areas, did not distinguish between physical and mental symptoms. In addition, some Eastern religions considered all illnesses to be due to offenses against gods or spirits; some religions mentioned sin specifically as the cause of all sickness. This was true of the Hittite religion, for example; and confession of sin to the priest-physician was the first step in treatment. If a patient could not recall or actually denied having sinned, he was required to recount his dreams to the priest-physician (3).

The idea of a connection between evil and psychiatric symptoms did not, of course, die out. An interesting example of a highly specific relation between evil on the one hand and depression and anxiety on the other is to be found in *De Anima* by Cassiodorus. Cassiodorus, who lived during the sixth century, is generally recognized as the scholar who did more than any other single person to keep learning alive during the Dark Ages in the barbarized West; the writings of both Cassiodorus and Cassian were required reading among scholars for centuries. *De Anima* contains a section called "How to recognize a bad man." It says:

> His face is clouded with evil, whatsoever his bodily grace. He is sad, even when making merry; later when repentance comes, deserted by the impulse of pleasure, he forthwith returns to sadness. His eyes move restlessly; as a second thought comes, he is unsteady, roving, shifty, a prey to anxiety, disturbed by suspicions. He is much influenced by others' judgements about himself, since in his folly he has lost all judgement of his own (4).

Cassian's idea that there is a relation between depression, boredom, and anxiety is of particular interest. However, Cassian's ideas about acedia were gradually submerged, and the condition came to be considered merely a subdivision or a variety of depression in which boredom and self-disgust occurred. Depression was, of course, another of the deadly sins. The writings of many medieval scholars and theologians, including St. Thomas Aquinas, included this definition of acedia.

In 1215 the fourth Lateran Council decreed a new emphasis on preaching to and confession by the laity; the varieties and derivatives of disgust with life in general were listed in detail: sorrow, laziness, weariness, spiritual negligence, lack of joy in general and particularly in prayer, despair in general and particularly of one's own salvation, doubt, grief, tedium, hatred of life. (It was considered sinful to be filled with sadness or disgust with God's world.)

Laymen either were incompletely aware of the writings of earlier philosophers or were less likely to be influenced by their authority than were medieval theologians. Accordingly, it is not surprising to find that one layman, Chaucer, gave acedia still another definition. In "The Persones Tale," Chaucer says: "After the synne of Envye and of Ire, now wol I speken of the synne of accidie." He goes on, "Envye and Ire make bitterness in herte; which bitterness is moder of Accidie." He also called it "ye anguish of a trouble heart making a man hevy thoughtful and wraive." (Wraive = crude, unsociable, irritable.) He recommends that "Agayns this roten-herted sinne of accedie and slouthe sholde men exercise hem-self to doon gode werkes and manly and vertuously cacchen corage well to doom." On the other hand, Caxton in his Order of Chyvalry said: "A man that hath accydye or slouthe hath sorrow and anger." (Anger = angor = anxiety.) Dante uses the word "accidioso."

Petrarch, who clearly suffered from acedia himself, gave it still another meaning (5). He himself manifested an important symptom that had never been mentioned in connection with acedia: an almost voluptuous pleasure in his own emotional sufferings. Another aspect of the syndrome that he unwittingly manifested was delight in exhibitionistic self-revelation, as shown in minutely detailed accounts of his own spiritual sufferings. Furthermore, he defined the condition not as a sin, but as a disorder brought on by consideration of the miseries of human life. Petrarch thus was the first to describe *Weltschmerz* in modern terms, and Goethe, Baudelaire, and others who later reveled in it were, whether they knew it or not, his followers. Moreover, Petrarch's unwitting additions to the list of manifestations of acedia moved the syndrome from the realm of theology to that of psychiatry. The psychiatric significance of acedia has been recognized by modern authors (6). Petrarch unwittingly changed the meaning of acedia so that it no longer connoted a sin but instead came to be regarded as a condition of positive value, that is, a state of mind that was essential to a contemplative life. This change was due not only to Petrarch's self-satisfied preoccupation with his own thoughts, but also to his ignorance of etymology and his scorn for Scholastic ideas.

The word acedia (or acidia, or accidia, or accidie) disappeared from common usage after the sixteenth century. Nevertheless, the earlier writings about it are of interest because they referred to psychiatric matters that are currently being discussed: in the first place, Cassian indicated that there was a relation between boredom and anxiety; in the second place, his predecessor Evagrius Ponticus and many of his followers emphasized that boredom might be a manifestation of depression; in the third place, Petrarch, through his solipsistic misinterpretation of the word, accidentally enunciated the ideas behind "beatnik" thinking.

John Cassian's writings on acedia were among the earliest and certainly among the best. His description of the anxious boredom of young scholars (reprinted on the next few pages), and how it stultified activity, thereby leading to an appearance of sloth, will sound familiar to today's advisors of college students.

REFERENCES

1. Cassian, John. *De Institutis Coenobiorum et de Octo Principalium Vitiorum Remediis.* Libri XII. In Migne, P. L., *Patrologiae cursus completus . . . .* Series Latina. Paris: Mogne, 1844–1880.
2. Bloomfield, M. W. *The seven deadly sins.* East Lansing: Michigan State University Press, 1952.
3. Gurney, O. *The Hittites.* London: Penguin Books, 1952.
4. Rand, E. K. *The founders of the Middle Ages.* New York: Dover Publications, 1957, p. 246.
5. Wenzel, S. Petrarch's accidia. *Studies in the Renaissance* 8:37–48, 1961.
6. Alphandéry, P. De quelques documents médiévaux relatifs à des états psychasthéniques. *Journal de Psychologie Normale et Pathologique* 26:763, 1929.

BOOK X. ON THE SPIRIT OF ACEDIA*

John Cassian

*From Nancy Wilson's translation.

I

The sixth battle for us is what the Greeks call acedia which we can render as weariness or anxiety of heart. This is related to depression and is a more pernicious and frequent enemy, greatly experienced by solitaries and dwellers in a hermitage, troubling the monk most greatly at about the sixth hour [noon], even like some fever, increasing at an appointed time, it brings the most burning waves of its approach at customary fixed hours on the diseased soul. Hence some of the elders say that this is the demon of noonday which is mentioned in the ninetieth psalm.

II

When it besieges a wretched mind, it begets repugnance for the place, loathing of the cell, and likewise the spurning and contempt by the negligent and less spiritual brothers who live near him. It makes him sluggish and inert toward every task within the wall of his cell; it does not let him dwell in his cell nor put his effort into reading, and he laments the more that he can do nothing, remaining a long time in this state, and that he has no spiritual fruit; till at length he has been joined to it in companionship; he complains and sighs and grieves that he stands empty of all spiritual seeking and idle in his place like one who although he could even rule others and surpass most, has built nothing nor has profited anyone with his speech and learning; he leaves the cell, with which he will feel about to perish if he remains in it, and whence he shall remove himself as fast as possible. Then the fifth and sixth hours arouse such great weariness of body and hunger for food, that he seems to himself as exhausted and weary as if with a long journey and most heavy labor, or as if he had refused food for a two-day fast. Then especially he looks around. He praises distant and far-removed monasteries, he describes them as places more useful and agreeable for salvation; also he pictures in the same place the company of the brothers, sweet and full of spiritual conversion. And, against this, all harsh things which exist here and not only that there is no building in which the brothers who live in the place, but that even the nutriment of the body is not obtained without great labor. . . . He looks more often toward the sun moving more slowly to its setting. And so by a kind of irrational confusion of mind as if he is filled with a black darkness, he is rendered idle and empty of every spiritual act, so that he thinks that there is no remedy for such an attack except for the visitation of a brother or the solace of sleep.

III

Thus the unhappy soul, attacked by such contrivances of her enemies is shaken, until, waried with the spirit of acedia which is like a most powerful battering ram, it learns either to fall into sleep, or, shaken out of his shell becomes accustomed to seek consolation for this onslaught in the visit of a brother. And this which is a weak remedy, afterward it becomes more weak. For the Adversary will tempt the man more frequently and more seriously, for the Adversary knows that the man is about to turn his back when battle starts and sees that the man hopes for safety not through victory and battle, but through flight. Meanwhile, drawn away little by little from his cell, he begins to be forgetful of his profession which is none other than the sensing and contemplation of that divine purity which excels all things, which cannot be achieved otherwise except in silence and constant perserverance in the cell, and meditation. Thus the soldier of Christ, made a fugitive and deserter of his regiment "involves himself in worldly things, and to Him (2 Tim. 2:4) for whom he has enlisted he is not well pleasing."

Chapter 6

THE SINGULAR CASE OF JAMES TILLY MATTHEWS

a clear paranoid

Diagram of the imaginary machines invented by his imaginary persecutors to torture Mr. Matthews in his imagination. (Compare with the cellar floor plan later in this chapter.)

In some cases of systematized delusions the psychotic ideas are limited to a single aspect of the patient's mental processes. In all other spheres he may be completely sane. Only when the sphere of his delusions is entered does he reveal his mental disease. Some such patients, warned by experience, avoid any conversation that might reveal their delusions, and pass for perfectly normal persons. These are the clear paranoids. They often create serious difficulties in diagnosis, and are unresponsive to treatment. They are likely to cause complicated medicolegal problems on occasions when they perform acts of violence or dispose of property unwisely. In the fields of politics or religion they may attract followers and, in some cases, may become either famous leaders or serious threats to the established systems. Their delusions of persecution may arouse organized sympathy. Their ideas of reference and of unique greatness may make them false messiahs or persecuted heretics. With respect to the last it is instructive to read accounts of judicial proceedings against such persons as those categorized as "free-spirits" in the late Middle Ages; many of them were clearly trying to reform a debauched system, but others were clearly mad.

The case report reprinted here is important for three reasons: One, the report by Haslam (1)—who also gave us the first detailed description of a patient with schizophrenia of the hebephrenic type—is the first, and for a long time was the only, detailed account of the disorder. Two, the patient was James Tilly Matthews. Matthews is discussed by Robert Darnton in his *Mesmerism and the End of the Enlightenment in France.* The

French Revolution permitted—and even encouraged—the activities of a host of nutty self-professed philosophers, some of whom were astrologers, others religious mystics, and the majority mesmerists. The mesmerists were convinced that the hypothetical mesmeric fluid that pervaded the universe could be directed to the minds of the people and their leaders, inducing them to formulate a political system that would provide the universal justice, permanent peace, and unending prosperity necessary for the complete happiness of all of humanity. Matthews, then living in France, was a mesmerist, but he played a special role. In 1794 Matthews claimed to have received, via the mesmeric fluid, messages that comprised peace proposals sent from London by the British government. The French Committee of Public Safety gave serious consideration to these purported proposals but did not accept them—not because they thought the method of transmission unbelievable but, rather, because Matthews' politics were suspect. The committee jailed him for Dantonist deviations (2).

The third reason for considering this case important is the typical manner in which the patient fooled people. Not only were the French authorities perfectly willing to accept his delusions as realities, but later, in England, he also fooled two leading clinicians, the famous Clutterbuck and the outstanding Birkbeck. Their discussions with Matthews evidently did not enter the sphere of his delusional system, for they pronounced him sane and recommended his release from Bethlem. Matthews' delusions sound completely modern today: foreign (Russian!) spies, plots against government figures, a wonderful machine that transmits thoughts and forces the recipient to have bad thoughts, forced behavior, bad smells, seminal fluid, electric forces, voices in different parts of the body, peculiar pains—all for the purpose of making the mysteriously chosen victim suffer physically and mentally.

REFERENCES

1. Haslam, J. *Illustrations of madness: Exhibiting a singular case of insanity.* . . . London: G. Daires, 1810.
2. Darnton, R. *Mesmerism and the end of the Enlightment in France.* Cambridge, Mass.: Harvard University Press, 1968, p. 131.

ILLUSTRATIONS OF MADNESS*

J. Haslam

PREFACE

The publication of the following case is deemed as much an act of justice, as it may be regarded a matter of curiosity. It may possibly effect some good, by turning the attention of medical men to the subject of professional etiquette, and to a consideration of those nice feelings and reciprocal charities, which confer on the practitioners of medicine the amiable distinction of a fraternity.

If it should merely succeed in curbing the fond propensity to form hasty conclusions, or tend to moderate the mischief of privileged opinion, the purpose is sufficiently answered.

From the temperate exposure of facts which the Writer has adopted, it can never be supposed that his views are hostile. The Brethren are unknown to him, and probably may never condescend to notice him beyond an occasional recollection: but if, contrary to his expectation, the Reader, throughout this narrative, should suspect a sneer, the benevolence of the Writer allows him to soften and correct it by a smile.

Of the history and opinions of the Insane, much curious matter is dispersed, and might advantageously be collected from works of various descriptions: most authors (generally without design) have contributed something; and if such scattered materials were gleaned into a volume, the "Use and Improvement of Madness in a Commonwealth" might be sooner and more clearly ascertained.

In Germany, Mr. Spiess has published four volumes of the biography of insane persons[†], which have been perused with much interest, and deserve to be rendered into English: and in our own country there exists a learned monument of madness,

---

*The following report is from Haslam, J. *Illustrations of Madness: Exhibiting a Singular Case of Insanity.* . . . London: G. Daires, 1810.

[†]Biographien der Wahnsinnigen, von Krist. Heinrich Spiess, Leipzig, 1795.

distinguished by abrupt transitions, a generous reconciliation of discordant circumstances, with a felicitous remembrance of transactions that never occurred, and which constitute the broad features of genuine insanity. That the reader may duly appreciate the labours of this gentleman, an extract is submitted to his candid consideration*.

"I conclude with offering an interpretation of a few lines from a part of the 3d Aeneid, which, according to what is said in my former Notes, p. 140, to which Notes I again here refer, has a particular relation to the whole of this subject:

Corripio è stratis corpus, tendoque supinas
Ad coelum cum voce manus, et munera libo
Intemerata focis: perfecto laetus honore
Anchisen facio certum remque ordine pando.
Agnovit prolem ambiguam geminosque parentes
Seque novo veterum deceptum errore locorum.
Tum memorat—

the meaning of which I venture to unriddle as follows: supposing (to speak as Virgil does, in the first person) I have a patient attacked by a contagious pestilential disease (its contagion being implied by the litter of staw, è stratis, in which he lies), I take up his body from thence, without a moment's delay (corripio), and curry it (corripio), or tan it (tendo), from the back and spine (as implied perhaps by the French dos, tergum, in tendo, and by supinas) to the poll or hollow part of the head (that hollow part being pointed to by the Greek word κοιλον, idem quod coelum), or, in other words, by administering the bark externally to those parts (the bark being implied in the word manus, by a reference to the Andes), as the patient lies supine, with his face turned to the skies, in a bath which comes level with his mouth (cum voce), the great heat of which bath is denoted by (focis), as its containing an infusion of purifying aromatic herbs may be by (munera intemerata), though these

---

*Vide "A Supplement to Notes on the Ancient Method of Treating the Fever of Andalusia, now called the Yellow Fever, deduced from an Explanation of the Hieroglyphics painted upon the Cambridge Mummy, by Robert Deverell, Esq. M. P. May 19, 1806," page 38. It is a subject of regret that these scarce and luminous pages were privately printed.

words, as coupled with (libo), should at the same time seem to imply the patient's drinking a quantity of hot tea (implied perhaps by te, in intemerata). After he has thus lain in the bath a full hour (perfecto honore) with the fires that heat it well lighted, or strongly burning (laetus); I produce the effect of ensuring (facio certum) the ague-fit (implied by Anchisen, near the ice, or a fit nearly allied to ice in its nature), and thus in due order acquire a key to the fever (remque ordine pando); or these last words may perhaps imply (and then in due order resort to the use of cathartics). Of the next two lines, the first seems to intimate that the patient, in consequence of such a process, shews the twofold nature of his complaint, cold and hot, ague and fever; and the second, when coupled with the context, that the disease is contracted by a change of climate, viz. that of Europe for that of the West Indies. The two last words (tum memorat) intimate that, when the point of the process is attained, the bark (implied by a reference to the river Mamore, on which the tree producing it grows) is afterwards to be taken internally, in order to a completion of the cure."

That the author of the Andalusia and Supplement is a formidable rival to the specimen now to be produced, cannot in fairness be denied, but in the comparison some "partial fondness" induces me to think, that "the superiority must, with some hesitation, be allowed to Mr. Matthews." "If the flights of Matthews, therefore, are higher, Deverell continues longer on the wing. Matthews often surpasses expectation, and Deverell never falls below it."

It only remains to mention that these opinions have been collected from the patient since the termination of the legal proceedings; and to inform the intelligent reader that, where inverted commas are used, the manuscript of Mr. Matthews has been faithfully copied; and that, for thus introducing his philosophic opinions to the notice of a discerning public, he feels "contented and grateful."

JOHN HASLAM

Bethlem Hospital,
    Nov. 2, 1810.

ILLUSTRATIONS OF MADNESS

James Tilly Matthews, whose opinions chiefly form the subject of the following pages, was admitted a patient into Bethlem Hospital, by a petition from the parish officers of Camberwell, on the 28th of January, 1797. Although his insanity was then most evident, yet his relatives did not possess the faculty of perceiving his disorder. They employed an attorney, and by a legal process he was ordered on the second of May following to be brought to the dwelling house of the late Lord Kenyon, in Lincoln's Inn Fields, who, after conversing with him, was perfectly satisfied that he was a maniac, and desired him to be remanded to his former custody. On the 21st January 1798, he was placed on the incurable establishment. In this situation he continued for many years, sometimes, an automaton moved by the agency of persons, hereafter to be introduced to the notice of the reader; at others, the Emperor of the whole world, issuing proclamations to his disobedient subjects, and hurling from their thrones the usurpers of his dominions.

In the year 1809 his relatives again interfered, and confiding in their own opinion, that he was of sound mind, and possessed the proper direction of his intellects, requested that he might be discharged. They also made application to the Churchwardens and Overseers of the parish of Camberwell, who, in the first instance, had been compelled to confine him in consequence of an order from the magistrates of Bow Street. These parish officers visited the lunatic, and being competent judges of the subject, demanded his release, on the pretence that he was perfectly recovered.

To confirm their opinion of the rational state of Mr. Matthews, the relatives employed two learned and conscientious Physicians, gentlemen deeply conversant with this disease, and doubtless instructed by copious experience to detect the finer shades and more delicate hues of intellectual disorder.

After repeated and wary examinations of the lunatic's mind, narrowly scrutinizing into his most recondite opinions, and delving into the recesses of his thoughts, they pronounced him to be perfectly in his senses, and sanctified such decision by the following affidavit, and holy affirmation.

In the King's Bench

HENRY CLUTTERBUCK, of Bridge Street, Blackfriars, in the City of London, Doctor of Medicine, maketh oath and saith, that he hath had four* interviews of considerable length with James Tilly Matthews; at one* of which Doctor Munro was present; that this deponent could not discover any thing that indicated insanity in the said James Tilly Matthews, and he verily believes him to be perfectly sane.

HENRY CLUTTERBUCK

Sworn in Court, this ⎫
   Twenth-seventh Day ⎬
   of November, 1809. ⎭

By the Court.

*See (*) below.

In the King's Bench

GEORGE BIRKBECK, of Cateaton Street, in the City of London, Doctor of Medicine, upon his solemn affirmation saith, that he hath paid six visits professionally to James Tilly Matthews, now under confinement in Bethlem Hospital. That during these visits he has attempted by every mode of examination which he could devise, to discover the real state of the mind of the said James Tilly Matthews, and that the result of such repeated, careful, and unprejudiced examinations, has been a conviction, that the said James Tilly Matthews is not insane. That in order to corroborate or to rectify this conclusion, he applied to Dr. Munro, the Physician to the Hospital aforesaid, for information, whether, by his knowledge and observation of the said James Tilly Matthews, he had been put in possession of any particular subject or subjects, which, on being mentioned within his hearing, did produce maniacal hallucination, and which this affirmant might not have been enabled to discover in the course of these conferences with Mr. Matthews? to which question Doctor Munro replied, that he was not acquainted with any such subject, but that he believed him to be insane upon all. To render this investigation more satisfactory and conclusive to this affirmant, it was agreed, that on the following Saturday he should meet the said Doctor Munro together, to see and converse with Mr. Matthews. This meeting took place accordingly; Doctor Clutterbuck (who accompanied this affirmant professionally in four* of the visits before mentioned)* being also present. That neither in this conference, nor in a conversation with Dr. Munro immediately subsequent thereto, (Mr. Matthews having left the room in which it took place) did any thing occur to alter the opinion of this affirmant as already expressed; but, on the contrary, that opinion was strengthened by these communications. And this affirmant further saith, that the said Dr. Munro, after finding the reasons advanced by him for the purpose of establishing the insanity of Mr. Matthews unsatisfactory to this affirmant's mind, did, near the conclusion of the interview above mentioned, declare, that although he might not succeed in convincing them, (Doctor Clutterbuck and this affirmant) or any other person, that Mr. Matthews was deranged, he had a feeling on which he could rely, that Mr. Matthews was insane, or words of the same import. And this affirmant further saith, that the most prominent circumstances adduced in proof of the insanity of Mr. Matthews, referred to parts of his protracted confinement, not including with the last six years, with the exception of his inflexible resistance to the admission of his alleged insanity, and to the customary expression of thanks for the benefits received in the hospital, together with his unabated antipathy against the physician and apothecary, to whose care he had been entrusted during his long confinement. That the circumstances stated were not, in this affirmant's judgment, sufficient proofs of insanity, and therefore it is still the opinion and belief of this affirmant, that the mind of the said James Tilly Matthews is sound.

GEORGE BIRKBECK

Affirmed in Court, this
   Twenty-seventh Day
   of November, 1809.

By the Court.

Thus armed, the relatives moved for a Habeas Corpus, in order that the said J.T.M. should be discharged.

It may here be proper to state that it had been the unvarying opinion of the medical officers of Bethlem Hospital, that Mr. Matthews had been insane from the period of his admission to the present time. Such opinion was not the result of casual investigation; but a conclusion deduced from daily observation during thirteen years. But aware of the fallibility of human judgment, and suspecting that copious experience which sheds the blessings of light upon others, might have kept them in the dark: perhaps startled at the powerful talents, extensive learning, and subtile penetration which had recorded in the face of day the sanity of a man whom they considered as an incurable lunatic: and flinching at an oath contradictory to such high testimony, the medical officers prudently referred the determination of the case to the constituted and best authorities in the kingdom. For this purpose they assembled a consultation of eminent medical practitioners, who, after a deliberate examination of the patient's mind, made oath in the following manner:

In the King's Bench

SIR LUCAS PEPYS, of Upper Brook Street, Grosvenor Square, in the County of Middlesex, Bart. Doctor of Medicine, Physician to His Majesty, President of the College of Physicians, and one of the Commissioners for visiting insane patients at private houses;

ROBERT DARLING WILLIS, of Tenterden Street, Hanover Square, Doctor of Medicine, Fellow of the Royal College of Physicians;

SAMUEL FOART SIMMONS, of Poland Street, in the County of Middlesex, Doctor of Medicine, Physician to St. Luke's Hospital;

RICHARD BUDD, of Craven Street, in the Strand, Doctor of Medicine, Elect and Treasurer, and one of the Fellows of the Royal College of Physicians, and also one of the Commissioners for visiting insane patients as aforesaid;

HENRY AINSLEY, of Dover Street, Piccadilly, Doctor of Medicine, Fellow of the Royal College of Physicians, and one of the Commissioners as aforesaid;

JAMES HAWORTH, of Bedford Row, in the County of Middlesex, Doctor of Medicine, Fellow of the College of Physicians, and one of the Commissioners as aforesaid;

WILLIAM LAMBE, of the King's Road, Bedford Row, Doctor of Medicine, Fellow of the Royal College of Physicians, and one of the Committee as aforesaid, (being the whole of the Commissioners appointed by the Royal College of Physicians for visiting insane persons at private houses;)

RICHARD POWELL, of Essex Street, in the Strand, Doctor of Medicine, Fellow of the Royal College of Physicians, and Secretary to the said Commissioners;

Severally make oath and say, that they had, on Wednesday, the 29th day of November instant, a long examination of the patient, James Tilly Matthews, at Bethlem Hospital, and that they took considerable pains in ascertaining the state of his mind, and that it is their positive and decided opinion, as the result of such examination, that the patient is in a most deranged state of intellect, and wholly unfit to be at large.

Sworn at my Chambers, Serjeant's Inn, by

SIR LUCAS PEPYS,
ROBERT DARLING WILLIS,
SAMUEL FOART SIMMONS,
RICHARD BUDD,
HENRY AINSLEY,

JAMES HAWORTH,
WILLIAM LAMBE,
RICHARD POWELL,

the above-named Deponents, this 30th Day of November, 1809, before me,

S. Le BLANC

This corroboration of Mr. Matthews' insanity, by the highest and most respectable testimony, gave a different complexion to the case, and also suggested some reflections.

Madness being the opposite to reason and good sense, as light is to darkness, straight to crooked, &c. it appears wonderful that two opposite opinions could be entertained on the subject: allowing each party to possess the ordinary faculties common to human beings in a sound and healthy state, yet such is really the fact: and if one party be right, the other must be wrong: because a person cannot correctly be said to be *in* his senses and *out* of his senses at the same time.

But there is considerable difficulty and some danger in applying logic to facts. Every person who takes the degree of Doctor becomes, in consequence of taking such degree, a learned man; and it is libellous to pronounce him ignorant. It is true, a Doctor may be blind, deaf and dumb, stupid or mad, but still his Diploma shields him from the imputation of ignorance.* It has also not unfrequently occurred, that a man who has been dubbed a Doctor of Medicine at Leyden, Aberdeen, or St. Andrews, and whose Diploma sets forth his profound learning, accomplishments, and competence to practise on the lives of His Majesty's good and faithful subjects, has been found incapable of satisfying the gentlemen in Warwick Lane that he possessed the common rudiments of his profession, and has been by them accordingly rejected: so that learning in many instances appears to be local.

Presuming Drs. Birkbeck and Clutterbuck to be very learned in their profession, and, if possible, still more learned out of it, uniting many rare talents, and distinguished by extrinsic acquisitions,

*The feeblest intellect I ever commiserated was a Doctor of Laws from the University of Glasgow.

"Grammaticus, Rhetor, Geometres, Pictor, Aliptes
"Augur, Schoenobates, Medicus, Magus—"

Conceding so much, it should follow, that if Mr. Matthews were mad, Messrs. Birkbeck and Co. ought to have discovered it; but the admission of such an inference would be destructive of their veracity: for had they found him to be a madman, it is to be hoped they never would stiffly and point blank have sworn him to be in his senses. How they could fail to detect his insanity is inexplicable, as his disorder was evident to all who saw and conversed with him; even his fellow-*students** derided the absurdity of his doctrine:—however, it should be recollected that these gentlemen have much practical experience, and are competent judges of all systems of error but their own.

It appears, these Doctors generally visited him in conjunction: perhaps they might have succeeded better, if they had examined him separately; for it is within the range of possibility that the judgment may have been warped by the courtesy, or clouded by the formality of a consultation—

"As two spent swimmers,
"That do cling together, and choke their art."

It may here be allowable to state, that if Drs. Birkbeck and Co. had, in the first instance, made application to the medical officers of the hospital, and announced their object, they would have been received with the urbanity due to professional gentlemen, and furnished with every information; but they preferred a silent approach and secret inquisition.

In the ordinary language of our courts of law, the relatives took nothing by their motion; nor is it my intention to bestow a single sentence on their conduct—the practice of the two Doctors shall be left to the humane construction of the Christian reader; and to finish the paragraph, the churchwardens and overseers of the parish of Camberwell may be supposed to have acted most conscientiously; and that the convenience of being disburthened of a pauper lunatic never entered their thoughts.

*Is any *student* tearing his straw in piece-meal, swearing and blaspheming, biting his grate, foaming at the mouth, &c.—*Vide Tale of a Tub, page* 178, *edit.* 1704.

I shall now proceed to develop the peculiar opinions of Mr. Matthews, and leave the reader to exercise his own judgment concerning them.

Mr. M. insists that in some apartment near London Wall, there is a gang of villains profoundly skilled in Pneumatic Chemistry, who assail him by means of an Air Loom. A description of this formidable instrument will be given hereafter; but he is persuaded that an account of it is to be found in Chambers's Dictionary, edited by Dr. Rees in 1783, under the article *Loom*, and that its figure is to be seen in one of the plates relating to Pneumatics.

It is unnecessary to tell the reader that he will fruitlessly search that work for such information.

The assailing gang consists of seven members, four of whom are men and three women. Of these persons four are commonly resident, and two have never stirred abroad since he has been the subject of their persecution. Of their general habits little is known; occasionally they appear in the streets, and by ordinary persons would be taken to be pick-pockets or private distillers. They leave home to correspond with others of their profession; hire themselves out as spies, and discover the secrets of government to the enemy, or confederate to work events of the most atrocious nature. At home they lie together in promiscuous intercourse and filthy community.

The principal of this crew, is named Bill, or the King: he formerly surpassed the rest in skill, and in the dexterity with which he worked the machine: he is about 64 or 5 years of age, and in person resembles the late Dr. De Valangin, but his features are coarser; perhaps, he is a nearer likeness to the late Sir William Pultney, to whom he is made a duplicate. It was on account of something worked by this wretch, that another, by the force of *assailment**, actuated Rhynwick Williams to the commission of his monstrous practices. He also took Hadfield in tow, by means of magnetic impregnations, and compelled him to fire the Pistol at His Majesty in the theatre: but on this subject

*This term, which frequently occurs, and is not to be found in our dictionaries, either originates with Mr. M. or is extracted from the vocabulary of the pneumatic gang.

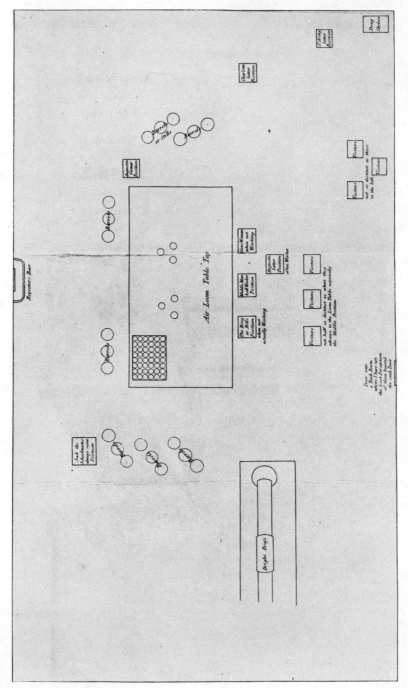

Floor plan of the cellar in which his imaginary persecutors worked to torture Mr. Matthews in his imagination. Original caption read, "Diagram or plan of the cellar, or place where the assassins rendezvous and work, showing their own, and the apparatus's relative positions, as it has at all times appeared to me by the sympathetic perception." (Compare with the diagram of the machines at the beginning of this chapter.)

there is a difference of opinion, as some of the female part of the gang attribute this event to *Blue-Mantle*, of whom nothing farther is known. In working the machine Bill exerts the most unrelenting and murderous villainy; and he has never been observed to smile.

The next in order, is a being called *Jack the Schoolmaster*, who is the short-hand-writer to the gang: he styles himself the recorder; somewhat tall, and about 60 years of age. It is not well ascertained if he wears a wig, but he generally appears in the act of shoving his wig back with his forefinger, and frequently says, "So you shall, when you can ketch (catch) us at it." Sometimes he says, "I'm to see fair play," and makes a merriment of the business. Jack has very seldom worked the machine.

The third person is *Sir Archy*, who is about 55 years of age, wears a drab-coloured coat, and, according to the old fashion, his breeches button between the legs. Some of the gang assert that Sir Archy is a woman dressed in men's apparel; and whenever Mr. Matthews has endeavoured, by enquiry, to ascertain this fact, Sir Archy has answered in a manner so quaint and indelicate that I cannot venture to communicate his reply. He is considered as the common liar of the gang; a low-minded blackguard, always cracking obscene jokes and throwing out gibes and sarcasms. In his speech there is an affectation of a provincial accent, so that when Mr. M. asserts the truth of any fact, Sir Archy replies yho (you) are misteaken (mistaken) He constantly stays in the apartment, and says he does not work the machine, but only uses a magnet. His mode of communicating with Mr. M. is principally by "*brain-sayings*," which term will be afterwards explained.

The last of the males is termed the *Middle Man*, who is about 57 years of age, of the middle stature, with a broad chest; has a twang of the hawk countenance, not pockfretten, and much resembling the late Mr. Smeaton, the engineer. He is dressed in a blue coat, with a plain waistcoat. It is said that he is a manufacturer of air-looms, and possesses the first rate skill in working this instrument. Altho' he is unrelenting in his persecution of Mr. M. he appears to consider it as sport, and sits grinning, apparently delighted that he cannot be taken unawares.

After his attacks, he generally observes that Mr. M. is the talisman; then Sir Archy replies, with a sneer, "Yes, he is the talisman."

Among the females who compose this establishment, *Augusta* may first be described. She is about 36 years of age, of the middle stature, and her countenance is distinguished by the sharpness of its features. In person she is not fleshy, nor can she be said to be a thin woman; she is not full-breasted. Ordinarily dressed, as a country tradesman's wife, in black, without powder. Augusta seldom works the machine, but frequently goes abroad to correspond with other gangs at the West end of the town. Of agreeable deportment, and at first seems very friendly and cajoling; but when she finds that she cannot influence and convince, becomes exceedingly spiteful and malignant. Her object is to influence women by her brain-sayings; and she states herself to be the chief of this department. Within the last seven years the virulence of her temper has been considerably exasperated.

Charlotte, the next in review, is about the same age as Augusta, and also of the middle stature, but more fleshy; has the appearance of a French woman, being a kind of ruddy brunette. She constantly stays at home with Sir Archy, and complains that she is forcibly confined to this situation. They keep her nearly naked, and poorly fed. Mr. Matthews is led to suppose that she is chained; for she has sometimes stated herself to be equally a prisoner with himself. Charlotte always speaks French, but her language and brain-sayings are conveyed in an English idiom. Her character is that of a steady, persevering sort of person, who is convinced of the impropriety of her conduct, but cannot help herself. For several years she has not worked the machine, but is a fixed and established reporter.

A very extraordinary lady compleats this malicious group. She does not appear to have any Christian name, but by the gang is termed the *Glove Woman*, as she constantly wears cotton-mittens. Sir Archy dryly insinuates that she keeps her arms thus covered because she has got the itch. She is about 48 years of age, is above the middle height, and has a sharp face. On her chin and upper lip there is a considerably quantity of fine downy hair, and she is somewhat pockfretten. Always dressed in a common fawn-coloured Norwich gown, with a plain cream-coloured camblet shawl, and wears a chip hat covered with black silk. The glove woman is remarkable for her skill in managing the machine. She frequently goes abroad. The rest of the gang, but particularly Sir Archy, are constantly bantering and plucking at her, like a number of rooks at a strange jack-daw: she has never been known to speak.

Having described the *dramatis personae*, it is expedient to mention the different preparations which are employed in the air-loom, by these pneumatic adepts, for the purposes of assailment.

Seminal fluid, male and female—Effluvia of copper—ditto of sulphur—the vapours of vitriol and aqua fortis—ditto of night-shade and hellebore—effluvia of dogs—stinking human breath—putrid effluvia—ditto of mortification and of the plague—stench of the cesspool—gaz from the anus of the horse—human gaz—gaz of the horse's greasy heels—Egyptian snuff, (this is a dusty vapour, extremely nauseous, but its composition has not been hitherto ascertained*)—vapour and effluvia of arsenic—poison of toad—otto of roses and of carnation.

The effects which are produced on Mr. Matthews by the skillful manipulation of these ingredients are according to his relation dreadful in the extreme. He has stated them in the technical language of the assailing gang, and explained their operation on his intellect and person. Whoever peruses a work on Nosology will be painfully impressed with its formidable catalogue of human miseries; it therefore becomes exceedingly distressing to swell the volume with a list of calamities hitherto unheard of, and for which no remedy has been yet discovered.

Fluid-locking.—A locking or construction of the fibres of the root of the tongue, laterally, by which the readiness of speech is impeded.

---

*This disgusting odour is exclusively employed during sleep, when, by their *dream-workings*, they have placed him, as a solitary wanderer, in the marshes near the mouth of the river Nile; not at that season when its waters bring joy and refreshment, but at its lowest ebb, when the heat is most oppressive, and the muddy and stagnant pools diffuse a putrid and suffocating stench;—the eye is likewise equally disgusted with the face of the country, which is made to assume a hateful tinge, resembling the dirty and cold blue of a scorbutic ulcer. From this cheerless scene they suddenly awake him, when he finds his nostrils stuffed, his mouth furred, and himself nearly choked by the poisonous effects of their Egyptian snuff.

Cutting soul from sense.—A spreading of the magnetic warp, chilled in its expansion, from the root of the nose, diffused under the basis of the brain, as if a veil were interposed; so that the sentiments of the heart can have no communication with the operations of the intellect.

Stone-making.—The gang pretend they can at pleasure produce a precipitation in the bladder of any person impregnated, and form a calculus. They boast of having effected this in a very complete manner for the late Duke of Portland.

Thigh-talking.—To effect this, they contrive so to direct their *voice-sayings* on the external part of the thigh, that the person assailed is conscious that his organ of hearing, with all its sensibility, is lodged in that situation. The sensation is distinctly felt in the thigh, and the subject understood in the brain.

Kiteing.—This is a very singular and distressing mode of assailment, and much practised by the gang. As boys raise a kite in the air, so these wretches, by means of the air-loom and magnetic impregnations, contrive to lift into the brain some particular idea, which floats and undulates in the intellect for hours together; and how much soever the person assailed may wish to direct his mind to other objects, and banish the idea forced upon him, he finds himself unable; as the idea which they have kited keeps waving in his mind, and fixes his attention to the exclusion of other thoughts. He is, during the whole time, conscious that the kited idea is extraneous, and does not belong to the train of his own cogitations.

Sudden death-squeezing; by them termed *Lobster-cracking.*— This is an external pressure of the magnetic atmosphere surrounding the person assailed, so as to stagnate his circulation, impede his vital motions, and produce instant death.

"In short, I do not know any better way for a person to comprehend the general nature of such lobster-cracking operation, than by supposing himself in a sufficiently large pair of nut-crackers or lobster-crackers, with teeth, which should pierce as well as press him through every particle within and without; he experiencing the whole stress, torture, driving, oppressing, and crush all together."

Stomach-skinning consists in rendering the stomach raw and sore, as if it had been scalded, and the internal coat stripped off.

Apoplexy-working with the nutmeg-grater consists in violently forcing the fluids into the head; and where such effort does not suddenly destroy the person, producing small pimples on the temples, which are raised, and rough like the holes in a nutmeg-grater: in a day or two they gradually die away.

Lengthening the brain.—As the cylindrical mirror lengthens the countenance of the person who views himself in such glass, so the assailants have a method by which they contrive to elongate the brain. The effect produced by this process is a distortion of any idea in the mind, whereby that which had been considered as most serious becomes an object of ridicule. All thoughts are made to assume a grotesque interpretation; and the person assailed is surprised that his fixed and solemn opinions should take a form which compels him to distrust their identity, and forces him to laugh at the most important subjects. It can cause good sense to appear as insanity, and convert truth into a libel; distort the wisest institutions of civilized society into the practices of barbarians, and strain the Bible into a jest book.

Thought-making.—While one of these villains is sucking at the brain of the person assailed, to extract his existing sentiments, another of the gang, in order to lead astray the sucker, (for deception is practised among themselves as a part of their system; and there exists no honor, as amongst thieves, in the community of these rascals) will force into his mind a train of ideas very different from the real subject of his thoughts, and which is seized upon as the desired information by the person sucking; whilst he of the gang who has forced the thought on the person assailed, laughs in his sleeve at the imposition he has practised.

Laugh-making consists in forcing the magnetic fluid, rarefied and subtilized, on the vitals, [*vital touching*] so that the muscles of the face become screwed into a laugh or grin.

Poking, or *pushing up the quicksilver.*—When the person assailed possesses an intellect sufficiently strong to be conscious of his impregnation, he naturally revolts at the atrocities practised upon him by the workers of this infernal machine, and becomes prompted to express his indignation at their perfidy. While in the act, as he supposes, of venting the burst of indignation, they contrive to push a seeming thread of fluid through his back diagonally in the direction of his vitals. Its operation is instantaneous, and the push appears to elevate the fluid about half an inch. This magic touch disarms the expression of his resentment, and leaves him an impotent prey to the malignity of their scorn and ridicule.

Bladder-filling is filling the nerves of the neck with gaz, and by continued distension, effecting a partial dislocation of the brain. This frequently repeated, produces weakness of intellect.

Tying-down; fettering the energy of the assailed's judgment on his thoughts.

Bomb-bursting is one of the most dreadful inflictions performed by the infernal agency of the air-loom. The fluid which resides in the brain and nerves, the vapor floating in the blood-vessels, and the gaz which occupies the stomach and intestines, become highly rarefied and rendered inflammable, occasioning a very painful distension over the whole body. Whilst the assailed person is thus labouring, a powerful charge of the electrical battery (which they employ for this purpose) is let off, which produces a terrible explosion, and lacerates the whole system. A horrid crash is heard in the head, and if the shock does not prove instantly fatal, the party only recovers to express his astonishment that he has survived the murderous attempt.

Gaz-plucking is the extraction of magnetic fluid from a person assailed, such fluid having been rarefied and sublimed by its continuance in the stomach and intestines. This gaz is in great request, and considered as the most valuable for the infernal purposes of these wretches. They contrive, in a very dexterous manner, to extract it from the anus of the person assailed, by the suction of the air-loom. This process is performed in a very gradual way, bubble by bubble.

The explanation of the forementioned terms will enable the reader sufficiently to understand others which belong to the science of assailment, as *foot-curving, lethargy-making, spark-exploding, knee-nailing, burning out, eye-screwing, sight-stopping, roof-stringing, vital-tearing, fibre-ripping*, &c. &c. &c.

The correspondence between Mr. M. and the members of this gang is kept up to a considerable extent by *brain-sayings*, which may be defined as sympathetic communication of thought, in consequence of both parties being impregnated with the magnetic fluid, which must be rarefied by frequent changing, and rendered more powerful by the action of the electrical machine. It is not hearing; but appears to be a silent conveyance of intelligence to the intellectual atmosphere of the brain, as subtilely as electricity to a delicate electrometer: but the person assailed (if he be sufficiently strong in intellect) is conscious that the perception is not in the regular succession of his own thoughts. The first hint Mr. M. received of the possibility of such sympathetic communication was in France, before the period of his confinement. He there, in one of the prisons, became acquainted with a Mr. Chavanay, whose father had been cook to Lord Lonsdale. One day, when they were sitting together, Mr. Chavanay said, "Mr. Matthews, are you acquainted with the art of talking with your brains?" Mr. M. replied in the negative. Mr. C. said, "It is effected by means of the magnet."

They likewise impart their thoughts to him by *voice-sayings*. This is an immediate conveyance of articulate sound to the auditory nerves, without producing the ordinary vibrations of air; so that the communication is intelligibly lodged in the cavity of the ear, whilst the bystander is not sensible of any impression.

Even during sleep they contrive to annoy him with their *dream-workings*, which consist in the power they exert of forcing their phantoms and grotesque images on his languid intellect. These assassins hold in their possession puppets of uncouth shape, and of various descriptions; by looking steadily at which they can throw the form into his brain, and thus render the perception more vivid to the dreamer; and the crafty solicitude with which they glean his waking opinions on the mysteries which, during the night, have danced in his imagination, is both wonderful and distressing.

On some occasions Mr. M. has been able to discern them; but whenever he has been watching their manoeuvres, and endeavouring to ascertain their persons minutely, they have appeared to *step back*, and eluded his search, so that a transient glimpse could only be obtained.

"Diffugient comites, et nocte tegentur opaca."

But the gang relate that they do not actually step back; but, at the moment when they are observed, that they grasp a metal which has the power of weakening the sympathy between them and the person assailed, and of benumbing his perception. This metal appears to be formed like a distaff or truncheon, and two such are fixed on the top of the machine. At the other times, they have pretended that each member of the gang is furnished with a separate metal.

The annexed figure of the air-loom, sketched by Mr. Matthews, together with *his* explanations, will afford the necessary information concerning this curious and wonderful machine.

References

"*a a.* The top of the apparatus, called by the assassins air-loom machine, pneumatic machine, &c. being as a large table.

"*b b.* The metals which the workers grasp to deaden the sympathy.

"*c.* The place where the pneumaticians sit to work the loom.

"*d.* Something like piano-forte keys, which open the tube valves within the air-loom, to spread or feed the warp of magnetic fluid.

"*e e.* Levers, by the management of which the assailed is wrenched, stagnated, and the sudden-death efforts made upon him, &c. The levers are placed at those points of elevation, *viz.* the one nearly down, at which I begin to let go my breath, taking care to make it a regular, not in any way a hurried breathing. The other, the highest, is where it begins to strain the warp, and by which time it becomes necessary to have taken full breath, to hold till the lever was so far down again. This invariably is the vital-straining. But in that dreadful operation by them termed lobster-cracking, I always found it necessary to open my mouth somewhat sooner than I began to take in breath: I found great relief by so doing, and always imagined, that as soon as the lever was at the lowest, (by which time I had nearly let go my breath) the elasticity of the fluid about me made it recoil from the forcible suction of the loom, much in the manner as a wave recoils or shrinks back after it has been forced forward on the sands in the ebbing or flowing of the tide: and then remains solely upon its own gravity, till the general flux or stress again forces it forward in form of a wave. Such appears to me the action of the fluid, which, from the time the lever being fully down, loses all suction-force upon it. I always thought that by so opening my mouth, which many strangers, and those familiar or about me, called sometimes singularity, at others affectation and pretext, and at others asthmatic, &c. instantly let in such momentarily emancipated fluid about me, and enabled me sooner, easier, and with more certainty, to fill my lungs without straining them, and this at every breathing.

"*f.* Things, apparently pedals, worked by the feet of the pneumaticians.

"*g.* Seemingly drawers, forming part of the apparatus as eudiometer, &c. &c..

"*h.* The cluster of upright open tubes or cylinders, and by the assassins termed their *musical glasses*, which I have so often mentioned, and perceived when they were endeavouring to burst my person, by exploding the interior of the cavity of the trunk. I now find an exact likeness in the Cyclopedia, which, being in electricity, is termed a battery.

"*i.* The apparatus mentioned as standing upon the air-loom, which the assassins were ever so watchful and active, by deadening the sympathy, to prevent my holding sight of; so that I could never ascertain what the bulky upper parts were, although the lower parts have appeared as distinct as the strength of the drawing shews. But I never had longer than the slow-glimpse-sight.

"*k l m.* The bulky upper parts, which, though always indistinct, appeared once or twice to be hid by an horizontal broad projection, and which has often made me query whether they rose through an aperture of the cellar ceiling into the room above, which the assassins' brain-sayings have frequently seemed to acknowledge.

"*n.* The windmill kind of sails I have so often mentioned, only seen by the glimpse of sympathy; and to prevent my judging of which, the assassins would dash with full strong sympathy or brain-saying, 'a whirligig,' used by children for amusement. But such windmill ever appeared as standing on the table.

"*o*. The barrels, which I perceived so distinctly after such long watching, to catch the sight of the famous goose-neck-retorts, which, by the assassins, are asserted to be about their loom, for supplying it with the distilled gazes, as well poisoned as magnetic, but which did not expose the goose-necks, which are here given, to shew the kind the assassins have, during ten years, some thousand times asserted they had: for while I was dwelling upon retorts themselves, which I had expected to find of metal, as stills, but which appeared distinctly hooped barrels standing on end on the floor, they cut the sympathy, and have ever since at all my attempts dashed or splashed the inward nerves of vision to bully and baffle me out of it.

"*p q r*. That part of the brass apparatus, so often seen distinctly of bright brass, standing on a one-step-high boarded floor, having a bright iron railing around it, the part not here shewn was never distinct.

"*s s*. The warp of magnetic-fluid, reaching between the person impregnated with such fluid, and the air-loom magnets to which it is prepared; which being a multiplicity of fine wires of fluid, forms the sympathy, streams of attraction, repulsion, &c. as putting the different poles of the common magnet to objects operates; and by which sympathetic warp the assailed object is affected at pleasure: as by opening a vitriolic gaz valve he becomes tortured by the fluid within him; becoming agitated with the corrosion through all his frame, and so on in all their various modes of attacking the human body and mind, whether to actuate or render inactive; to make ideas or to steal others; to bewilder or to deceive; thence to the driving with rage to acts of desperation, or to the dropping dead with stagnation, &c. &c. &c. Though so distinct to me by sympathy I have never caught the inward vision thereof, not even by glimpse; but the assassins pretend, when heated, that it becomes luminous and visible to them for some yards from the loom, as a weakish rainbow, and shews the colours according to the nature of the gazes from which it is formed, or wherewith the object is impregnated: as green for the copper-streams or threads, red for the iron, white for the spermatic animal-seminal, &c.

"*t*. Shews the situation of the repeaters, or active worriers, when such were employed during the active exertions so long made to worry me down.

"*u*. One of the assassins called by the rest Jack the Schoolmaster, who calls his exertions to prevent my writing or speaking correctly, *dictating*, he ever intruding his own style and endeavouring to force it upon me. He pretends to be the short-hand-writer, to register or record every thing which passes. He appears to have a seat with a desk some steps above the floor.

"V. The female of the gang called by the others Charlotte: she has always spoken French, even by her brain-sayings; but I yet doubt whether she be a French woman, though so much of that description of person, for frequently it is English-French: though this may be from *their* vocabulary being English and French combined.

"W. The one I call the common liar of the gang, by them termed Sir Archy, who often speaks in obscene language. There has never been any fire in the cellar where the machinery is placed.

"X. Suppose the assailed person at the greater distance of several hundred feet, the warp must be so much longer directly towards him, but the farther he goes from the pneumatic machine, the weaker becomes its hold of him, till I should think at one thousand feet he would be out of danger. I incline to think that at such distance or little more, the warp would break, and that the part nearest his person would withdraw into him, and that the next the loom would shrink into whatever there held it.

"Y. The middle man working the air-loom, and in the act of Lobster-cracking the person represented by the figure X.

"The assassins say they are not five hundred feet from me; but from the uncommon force of all their operations, I think they are much nearer."

They have likewise related that many other gangs are stationed in different parts of the metropolis who work such instrument for the most detrimental purposes. Near every public office an air-loom is concealed, and if the police were sufficiently vigilant, they might detect a set of wretches at work near the Houses of Parliament, Admiralty, Treasury, &c. and there is a gang established near St. Luke's Hospital. The force of assailment is in proportion to the proximity of the machine; and it appears that the interposition of walls causes but a trifling difference: perhaps at the distance of 1000 feet a person might be considered out of the range of its influence. Independently of the operation of this complex and powerful machine termed an Air-loom, which requires the person assailed to be previously saturated with magnetic fluid, a number of emissaries, who are termed *novices*, are sent about in different directions to prepare those who may hereafter be employed in the craft and mystery of event-working. This is termed *Hand-impregnation*, and is effected in the following manner: an inferior member of the gang, (generally a novice,) is employed in this business. He is furnished with a bottle containing the magnetic fluid which issues from a valve on pressure. If the object to be assailed be sitting in a coffee-house, the pneumatic practitioner hovers about him, perhaps enters into conversation, and during such discourse, by opening the valve, sets at liberty the volatile magnetic fluid which is respired by the person intended to be assailed. So great is the attraction between the human body and this fluid, that the party becomes certainly impregnated, and is equally bound by the spell as the lady was fixed to the chair of Comus, or the harmless fly is enveloped in the shroud of the spider.

In order to ascertain whether a person be impregnated, let him, fasting, imitate the act of swallowing, and if he should perceive a grating noise in his ears, somewhat resembling the compression of a new wicker-basket he is certainly attained.

In consequence of the numerous gangs established in this metropolis, all the persons holding high situations in the government are held impregnated. An expert of the gang, who is magnetically prepared, contrives to place himself near the person of a minister of state also impregnated, and is thus enabled to force any particular thought into his mind and obtain his reflections on the thought so forced.—Thus, for instance, when a Secretary at War is at church, in the theatre, or sitting in his office and thinking on indifferent subjects; the expert magnetist would suddenly throw into his mind the subject of exchange of prisoners. The Secretary would, perhaps, wonder how he became possessed of such a subject, as it was by no means connected with his thoughts; he would however turn the topic in his mind and conclude that such particular principle ought to form the basis of the negociation. The expert magnetist, having, by watching and sucking, obtained his opinion, would immediately inform the French Minister of the sentiments of the English Secretary, and by such means become enabled to baffle him in the exchange.

The same process would take place with the other ministers of state, and their opinions would be communicated to the enemy on the subjects of peace, commercial intercourse, or the fitting out of armaments. Let the plan be ever so well devised, the magnetists would be certain to paralize and bewilder the person chosen to command the expedition. This they effected in a very complete manner at Buenos Ayres, and still more recently in the Island of Walcheren.

Notwithstanding the dreadful sufferings which Mr. Matthews experiences from being assailed, he appears to derive some consolation from the sympathy which prevails between himself and the workers of the machine. Perilous as his present situation may be, it would be rendered still more alarming if he could not watch their proceedings, and thus be prepared to avert the force of their engine. This reciprocal impregnation and continuity of warp enables him to perceive *their* motions and attain *their* thoughts. Such seems to be the law of this sympathy, that mutual intelligence is the result; nor can the assailants, with all their skill and dexterity, deprive him of this corresponding perception. In proportion as their scientific advancement has instructed them in new and ingenious arts of tormenting, the progression of his experience has taught him to diminish the force of their attacks.

These assassins are so superlatively skillful in every thing which relates to pneumatic chemistry, physiology, nervous influence, sympathy, human mind, and the higher metaphysic, that whenever their persons shall be discovered, and their machine exhibited, the wisest professors will be astonished at their progress, and feel ashamed at their own ignorance. The gang proudly boast of their contempt for the immature science of the present aera.

Under all these persecutions and formidable assailments, it is the triumph of Mr. M. that he has been enabled to sustain himself; and this resistance has depended on the strength of his intellect and unremitting vigilance. Whenever he has perceived them about to make the wrench by suction, he has recoiled as one expecting to receive a blow shrinks back in order to avoid it. Without such ability and precaution he must long since have become the victim of bomb-bursting, lobster-cracking, or apoplexy-working with the nutmeg-grater.

Having described the machinery and actors in this "insubstantial pageant" it now only remains to afford some idea of the nature of *Event-working*, a science formerly supposed to depend on certain positions of the planetary system, and regulated by heads of houses in the university of the stars. Although much attention and some valuable time have been lost in becoming acquainted with this novel philosophy, yet after repeated trials and painful efforts, the writer has been unable adequately to explain the manner of working an event, particularly as the event is commemorated before it occurs. From these embarrassments he has been kindly relieved by Mr. Matthews, who has written down his ideas on the subject, and from whose manuscript the following pages are exhibited to the reader.

"The assassins opened themselves by their voices to me about Michaelmas 1798, and for several years called their infamies, *working feats of arms*, but seldom using the term *Event-working*: though after four or five years, when I, by perseverance, had beat them out of their insolence of assumption, (for they assumed the right of interfering with every body having heraldic bearings particularly, and for this part of their villainies called themselves the *efficient persons* to all those having titles to colleges of arms,) and *by* such titles also they used the term event-working for their actions.

"It is not an easy matter to define fully any regular instance of such, their called event-working, because they in everything introduced the names of some, or other personages, as concerned therewith, but who certainly, were not only ignorant of their very existence, but more or less victims to their abominations.

"However, to shew what the nature of such event-working is, namely, how infamous human beings, making a profession of pneumatic chemistry, and pneumatic magnetism, hire themselves as spies; and by impregnating persons, singled out by them as objects for interfering with, obtaining their secrets, actuating them in various ways, in thought, word and deed, as well as they can, to model their conduct, ideas or measures to favour the ends of assassin spies or event-workers, or their employers, &c. in bringing about which ends they sometimes are years and many years, varying from mode to mode from stratagem, and sometimes partially fail at last, according to the difficulty of getting near the object to operate upon, the strength of such person's nerves, brain, and personal affections, as well as nature of soul, &c. &c. The following, divested of their offensive introductions may suffice, being a few instances out of numberless events.

"While I was detained in Paris by the then existing French Government, during the years 1793-4-5, and beginning of 1796, I had even in the early part thereof, sufficient information, to be certain that a regular plan existed, and was furthering by persons in France, connected with persons in England, as well for surrendering to the French every secret of the British Government, as for the republicanizing Great Britain and Ireland, and particularly for disorganizing the British navy; to create such a confusion therein, as to admit the French armaments to move without danger.

"My sentiments having been resolutely hostile to every such plan, idea, and person assisting therein, proved, (as the assassins have ever avowed) the real cause of my having had Gens d'armes placed with me to prevent my return, and their having by such magnetic means of workers in Paris ascertained, that my said sentiments were so determined for the counteracting such plans, as well as others more dreadful in their nature, that I should persevere even to the loss of my life in my efforts to expose them. They have ever avowed also; that my having immediately on my return set about exposing the quoted infamies, occasioned a magnetic spy to be appointed from each gang of event-workers in London, specially to watch and circumvent me: for that the chiefs of such gangs were the real persons who were cloaked under certain names and titles used in the information given me, and which I have for years found such vile spy-traitor-assassins called by among their fraternity.

"That the persons mentioned by me in my letters, narratives, &c. to each of the 1796 administration, and to the then Speaker of the House of Commons as spies, whom I could not discover, but found, as it were, before me, and on every side of me, everywhere, and in everything (as was my expression) were magnetic spy-workers coming form Paris, at the time I was trudging it from thence, and having the charge of circumventing me; and such were so appointed by each of the London gangs, event-working assassins: who having found my senses proof against their fluid and hand-working as it is termed, were employed to actuate the proper persons to pretend I was insane, for the purpose of plunging me into a madhouse, to invalidate all I said, and for the purpose of confining me within the measure of the Bedlam-attaining-airloom-warp, making sure that by means thereof, and the poisonous effluvia they used, they would by such means keep me fully impregnated, and which impregnation could be renewable and aggravated at their pleasure, so as to overpower my reason and speech, and destroy me in their own way, while all should suppose it was insanity which produced my death.

"That not only such appointed spies, but the whole phalanx of event-workers, all the gangs rose up in arms against me; because all depended during that year (1796) on their disorganizing the British navy, which they had undertaken to effect, and had their experts at work to bring about; while my incessant and loud clamours, almost daily writing to, or calling at the houses of one or other of all the ministers in their turn, conjuring them to exert themselves to prevent wretches from disorganizing the British navy; this obliged such experts and gangs also, to have recourse to such caution till they could get rid of me; that in truth, they could not make any way therein while I was at large: and to this solely was owing their not having been able to fulfill their engagements with the French, to have the British fleet in confusion by the time stipulated; and which inability from such fear, more than the storm, forced General Hoche, whose armament was called the Avant-Garde of the intended French invasion to return as he came. And they have ever pretended that Hoche, having been exasperated against the workers, spoke bitterly of them, and was by one of their experts *put out*: (viz. destroyed by poisonous magnetic fluid, which kills by possessing itself of the hollows of the nerves, and does not affect the stomach, vitals, &c. as poysons in substance,) in order to prevent him from publishing the existence of the profession.

"That finding it much easier to actuate all the ministers, magistrates, &c. to the folly of pretending me mad, that to make me desist from exerting myself to expose the plots and plans of such assassins, they adopted this course, and at last contrived my being forced into Bedlam, where they have ever sworn, they will by hook or by crook hold me; and some thousand times during the last twelve years, sworn I should never get out of their clutches alive, unless I forgave them; but they know all compromise with them is impossible.

"That having me safely immured, the experts went to work again boldly, and then, in less than three months blew up that flame in the British navy, which threw the three great fleets into open mutiny, about Easter 1797: that this proving to the then ministry their danger, from their having mocked, and (by their tools, which as well as the ministers themselves, were tools in the hands of event-working assassins) imprisoned me; they then became so alarmed on the second mutiny of the Nore fleet, under Parker, a man actuated by magnet-working experts, that they opened the Treasury doors, and instead of attending to me, cost the nation near one hundred thousand pounds in secret service money, to quell the mutiny at the Nore, and prevent its again bursting out at Portsmouth, Plymouth, &c. and that to avoid the expenditure being noticed, as such, means were contrived to work it into the accounts, as for other purposes at earlier periods.

"It has ever been their custom to actuate every one to insult or ill-treat me: they could give their time to actuate, and then to swear to avenge it, and make a merit of event-working, to bring disgrace or injury upon such persons: never indeed, to benefit me; but as pursuing their systems of villainy, calling me their *Property* and *Talisman*, bringing persons under what they call their *Fluid-balances* against me; persecuting and making murderous efforts upon me: using the name or expression, or the presence of particular persons as their authority, and then pretending, because I with stood them, that they had a right against such persons, or whom they called such persons duplicates to.

"Hence they ever asserted that Mr. Pitt was not half able to withstand magnetic fluid in its operative effect, but became actuated like a mere puppet by the expert-magnetists employed in such villainies: that every one of his colleagues and successors to the present moment, have proved equally actuable, though some more, some less, Mr. Grey having proved the strongest, though not full proof: and pretending in their efforts to cajole me, that my having, (though not acquainted with him, and not withstanding his refusing to attend to *me* in 1796,) entertained a sort of friendly opinion for him, was the sole means of preserving his life when first Lord of the Admiralty, They say, that having read in my jumbled narratives the facts of traitor efforts to disorganize the navy, and even after the meeting, not only left me to linger here under their incessant murdering efforts, but accepted the office of first Lord of the Admiralty; the die was cast against him in their system of event-working, and he was to be *put out*, a term they use for their murdering any one. In truth, they did frequently say to me, when he took upon him the office, '*We have event-worked that; he is to be killed there*': and I mentioned it to several: but as all despised me and said it was insanity, I did not waste so much breath, together with pen, ink and paper, as I had done to expose the assassin's assertions respecting their *putting out* Mr. Pitt, which they truly effected.

"That the final order having been given to *put out* Mr. Grey by the pneumatic magnetists having in charge the Admiralty Department, for attaining its secrets, actuating its members, &c. the moment was determined on, and he actuated to be in a given place by the time. That this being well known as it proceeded, another magnetist contrived to puppet one of their prepared victims to be there also; and the fluid of this person (a Sir Michael Le Fleming,) having been rendered more attractive than Mr. Grey's; the wrench took hold of Sir Michael instead of Mr. Grey, and killed him on the spot; while, they say, by the force, Mr. Grey would have escaped with a rupture like the late Duke of Bedford, or the bursting of some blood-vessels which would not have produced death. Then they cried '*It's yho* (you) *that presearved* (preserved) *him*,' in their affected provincial jargon; for provincial is not their real language. During some weeks previous to this, they had been ripping at my ventricles by their air-loom-force: a dreadful operation it is! They pretended they worked Mr. Grey into the foreign office, where he might have the means of knowing the reality of the advances made by France to the British Government through *me* in 1793, and the folly of his chief friend Lord Grenville, thereupon, and then they said an expert was preparing a puppet to be actuated commemoratively, as Lord Grenville and his friends were to be made to act politically. Every time I saw the Philanthropic Insurance advertisements signed William Ludlam, which was daily, *they* would cry '*Voila le Victime*,' then '*That's his Ludship, Erskine, Grenville*,' and by brain-saying, refer to Mr. Erskine's mode of speech, for his Lordship pronouncing nearly Ludship, and say that William Ludlam meant William Lud Grenville, and touching the fluid in my vitals, would make me quite sorry. When Ludlam, pistol in hand, attempted to tyrant it over the master as well as the waiter of the London Tavern, they said '*It's exact. C'est ainsi*,' and to his jumping through the window also, they would cry '*C'est ainsi aussi*,' and '*Leighton, Sir William, we puppeted yho, there to commemorate.*' Some time after, when Ludlam was taken, Lord Erskine ordered him under the care of Dr. Monro, and prohibited the Lord Mayor's warrant from being served against him. *There* they would cry '*his Ludship*,' and then brainsay the subject as before. Then '*Ween*, (we will) *puppet yho also*,' and brainsay, '*We will actuate Erskine Monroish, yet.*' I mentioned their pretexts and sent out a memorandum thereupon, stating that, though they were active to prevent my perceiving all their drift, I feared they intended to make Lord Erskine mad; for they often asserted, that with but half stress on the fluid with which he was impregnated, he would become weak in intellect; and as it was to my wife, I could not help saying, 'Notwithstanding the readiness to act as Counsel for me in 1797, which Mr. Erskine professed, yet, when you called upon him to ask him from me to mention my case and imprisonment in Bedlam in the House of Commons, he would not do so; and for which the assassins boasted once they stagnated him in the House of Commons, by an air-loom warp, attaining him from no great distance; and would have killed him afterwards there as an example in their pretexts but for my exposing their infamous threats; he now cares no more for me than he does for the dogs in the street.' *'Enough* (they cried) *we'll shew you.'* At a subsequent time when it was said that the Lord Chancellor, passing along Holborn, saw several persons pursuing and beating a dog in order to kill him, pretending he was mad; *'Aye,* (they cried) *that's as you say we pursue you pelting you with our murdering efforts,'* but he not thinking any madness appeared about him, ran into the midst of them, and taking the dog up in his arms, rescued him from their fury, and ordered him to be conveyed to his stables and taken care of: *'Yes,* (said they) *that part is the derision of the event; we have commemorated your words; he does care about the dog, but you may lie in the stable* (a term used by them for being placed on the incurable establishment in Bedlam) *and be damned.'*

"When the change of Ministry came about, then they asked, *'Now where's poor Ludlom?'* He was actuated to a thought, that, with pistols pointed to them, he could force the parties to yield to him; but the good sense of the master of the tavern left him no alternative but to jump through the window and be off—brainsaying, that Lord Grenville and Co. were also endeavouring to establish their philanthropic assurance to the Catholics, thinking to make as much more than legal interest thereby, as Lud-lam and his partizans did by their philanthropic assurance, to gain them 8 per cent, besides bonuses frequently; and as Lud-lam had first opponents in his own party or subscribers, and then for his pistolling was forced through the window, so Lord Grenville, after having endeavoured to force the *Master* to comply with his wishes, was in turn forced through the window into the street, a term among them for *turned out.* Lud Erskine and some others were Lord Grenville and Co's. opponents in the cabinet to the philanthropic efforts to make more than common interest. They pretended they worked Ludlam into Dr. Monro's hands, as completing the event of my being in them: asserting, that the working the former Administration out, and Lord Grenville in, the rendering all their measures abortive, and then pushing them on to be turned out, was to commemorate and retaliate upon them, for their parts in the persecution and imprisonment I experienced."

Second Event-Working

"I ought not to omit mentioning, that about three or four years since, when the assassins so much boasted that a great deal of fluid prepared by them was sent to impregnate the *Mollys* as they termed *Mollendorf*, Brunswick, Kamenskoi, &c. to make fools of them in the battles the event-workers were working to produce: they said Russia must be weighed by me, crying, '*We told you that you were Buonaparte's talisman, and that we would work him up to as high a pitch of grandeur by the possession of you, as we would fix you degraded below the common level of human nature,*' (an expression often indeed used by them in menacing me during the years they so threatened to murder my son and all my family, if I would not forgive them: and would not only counteract me in every thing, but make every person presenting himself mock and ridicule me, and kill me at last, either secretly or openly, for that I should never escape out of their clutches alive; and after having asserted they would bring Russia to the balances for a few months, they cried '*Yho are coming,*' brainsaying, that a magnetic fluid impregnated Russian was coming. Soon it was announced through Bedlam, that some of the Royal Family were coming—preparations were made to receive them, when, lo! as the party entered the gallery, while the assassins were crying, '*Now for it, we will play you off,*' brainsaying, they should actuate him while they tortured me. One of the patients came to tell me that it was not any of the Royal Family, but the Duke of Somerset and the Russian Ambassador who were coming down. '*Aye, aye!* (said the assassins) *we told you we would give you notice,*' and began to torture and fluid-lock me, viz. binding all the small nerves and fibres so numerous about the parts composing the root of the tongue, which prevents regularity of speech, and forces me to speak rather slower and to be guarded at every word to prevent stammering. When the party came to my cell, five or six of them, I began to explain to them the manner in which I was assailed, and describe to them the nature of it, enquiring if they understood Pneumatic Science, &c. His Grace was with his left arm on the corner of my bed, and the party generally, politely attentive; but one of them attracted my notice from his seeming to become a little restless, going out of the cell, and not attending to what I was stating. The assassins said, '*That's the victim.*' A few days after, I learned that this person was the Russian Count Pahlin; the assassins chuckling, often asked me if I remembered the Russian with arms too short for his person, and an impediment in his speech, saying, '*It will be all over with the Mollys.*' Every thing was then quiet, but it was not long before Prussia began to be agitated, and this brought on the war which beat it and the Russians out of the field, and left the Count Pahlin dead upon it."

By this time it is probable that the curiosity of the reader is sufficiently satisfied concerning the mischievous and complicated science of event-working. Although the fable may be amusing, the moral is pernicious. The system of assailment and working events deprives man of that volition which constitutes him a being responsible for his actions, and persons not so responsible, in the humble opinion of the writer ought not to be at large. After the commission of murder or treason, it would be considered an inadequate defence for the perpetrator to allege that he had been irresistibly actuated by the dexterous manoeuvres of Bill, or the Middle man; nor is it at all probable, that the accurate records of Jack the Schoolmaster would be admitted as evidence in a court of law.

There are already too many maniacs allowed to enjoy a dangerous liberty, and the Governors of Bethlem Hospital, confiding in the skill and integrity of their medical officers, were not disposed to liberate a mischievous lunatic to disturb the good order and peace of society. These gentlemen can have no advantage in detaining a person in confinement who has recovered his senses. Their interest consists in the numbers who are restored to the community and their friends; and their only reward the incense which Gratitude projects on the altar of Reason.

FINIS

Chapter 7

THE EARLY HISTORY OF PSYCHIATRIC TREATMENT

Early nineteenth-century shock treatments for mental disease.

(Left) *Centrifuging the patient, a form of treatment widely established in Europe and used in New England up to about mid-century.*

(Right) *"The surprise bath." In this era any bath was a surprise, often a terrifying one.*

In an era in which much of the treatment used by physicians was superstitious (this era has not yet ended), it is to be expected that the treatment of mental disorders will also be found to be superstitious. There is no need for a detailed analysis of the vast amount of material on this kind of treatment of mental disease, however quaint and fascinating some of it may be. There are, however, certain items that are not only interesting but significant for today's psychiatry. But before discussing these matters, it is worth noting that the general care given patients must have had some influence on the results of specific treatments. The fragmentary data bearing on this point have been reviewed, at least for the early nineteenth century, by Dr. Otto M. Marx (1). One of the most important psychiatric discoveries of all time was the introduction of the flexible rubber stomach tube for feeding recalcitrant patients. It saved innumerable lives. An English physician, J. B. Steward, introduced it in 1845 (2).

The present essay will be limited to (1) psychotherapies, including suggestion, dream interpretation, and logotherapy; (2) milieu therapy; and (3) shock therapy. No more than passing mention will be made of drug therapy (of interest because in the past it included opium, chiefly for the relief of agitated depression) and of trephining (of interest because it began in prehistory and probably ended only recently (3).

THE PSYCHOTHERAPIES

The psychologic treatment of mental disorders has a long history, as does the treatment of all other illnesses. The earliest recorded history, that of the Mediterranean civilizations, reveals ideas that are essentially the same as those that obtain among primitive peoples of modern times.

The Psychotherapy of Demons

Laín Entralgo discusses the ancient Greek ideas in marvelously documented detail (4). The prevailing belief held that all illnesses of any sort were caused by the entry of a *daimón* into some part of the body. In those cultures psychotherapy was directed to the demon and not to the patient. By means of either ordinary words or gibberish, spoken, chanted, or sung with musical accompaniment, the demon was to be frightened, deceived, or persuaded to leave the patient. The musical instrument that would be used was the lyre, since the music of pipes was believed to have an adverse effect (5). (In later eras, the demon-container was sometimes beaten or half-drowned in order to convince the demon that it would be more comfortable elsewhere.) Whatever the means used, the general approach was usually reported to be successful. This therapeutic method was deficient in one respect, however: it made no provision for the residence of the expelled demon; it might enter another victim. This defect was remedied by the Christians, who removed the demons to the bodies of swine. On occasion, instead of making a demon's human residence uncomfortable, more startling measures were resorted to for its removal, as when Origen castrated himself in order to remove a demon that tormented him. Although Origen is referred to as an Early Christian Father, this event places the title in some doubt.

The psychotherapy of demons was abandoned for the most part by the nineteenth century, although it is still practiced by an occasional psychoanalyst (6).

In the early Christian era certain saints were believed to be especially efficient in the removal of demons that caused mental disorders; these were Avertin, Ruffin, and Vitus. St. Hilary of

Poitiers is perhaps of more current interest: a possessed person had only to lie on the saint's couch to be cured of his madness, in a manner reminiscent of what some believe happens today.

Suggestion

Another method of psychotherapy also dates back centuries. This is the use of suggestion. The charms, amulets, holy relics, and the like that were used so successfully in early eras were replaced by scientific devices that had similar effects. In the early nineteenth century suggestion often involved the use of magnets or objects believed to be magnets. Actually, the practice of suggestion by means of magnets had begun centuries earlier. Lodestones were used for treating a wide variety of conditions in medieval times, and lay healers used magnets during the Renaissance (7). Magnetism is said to have had its first use in medicine by Cardan in 1584 when he anesthetized a patient by touching him with a magnet. The idea that the human body had magnetic properties apparently was first enunciated by Paracelsus, who believed that healthy people possessed a strong

Paracelsus, an impatient activist who destroyed then-current medical superstitions and introduced his own. Mesmerism grew out of some of his ideas

magnetism and that illness was characterized by weakness of this magnetism—a state that could be treated by the application of magnets. Paracelsus believed that magnetism emanated from the planets and that this could beneficially be absorbed by man. When William Gilbert, president of the Royal College of Physicians and physician to Queen Elizabeth I, wrote his great treatise *De Magnete* in 1600, his published experiments exploded the idea that magnets cured diseases. Accordingly, most reputable physicians thereafter did not use magnets for therapeutic purposes, but mystics and quacks continued to do so. In the late eighteenth century Elisha Perkins of Connecticut invented a number of metallic instruments that were said to cure almost anything when applied appropriately; he and his son, who assisted him in the exploitation of these "magnetic tractors," became immensely wealthy.

The Perkinses are now, of course, universally recognized as quacks. Somewhat different is the case of Anton Mesmer of Switzerland, who, during the eighteenth century, originated the modern version of the doctrine of Animal Magnetism. He is considered a quack by most physicians, but a small group of psychoanalysts regard him as one of the founders of their craft. Mesmer's doctoral thesis at the University of Vienna was titled *The Influence of the Planets in the Cure of Disease*. In it he tried to prove that the sun, the moon, and the planets acted upon living beings by means of a subtle fluid called "Animal Magnetism" (7). His ideas were a direct plagiarism of some of Mead's writings. Mesmer was also greatly influenced by Fr. Hell, a Jesuit professor of astronomy who claimed to be able to effect cures through the application of metallic objects. It is also probable that Mesmer borrowed certain of his ideas from some of the more mystical works of Van Helmont, who as early as 1630 had stated (7): "The name magnetism is given to the occult influence that bodies exert on each other at a distance. . . . Magnetism acts everywhere and there is nothing new in it but the name." Mesmer also used older, more hackneyed concepts; he defined disease in general as "l'aberration de l'harmonie" and explained the origin of mental disease as follows: "L'irritabilité exagérée des nerfs produite par l'aberration de l'harmonie dans le corps humain est ce qu'on appelle plus particulièrement *maladies nerveuses.*" He claimed that "l'action du Magnétisme arrête l'abberration de l'état de l'harmonie."

It is unnecessary to describe in detail the multitude of magnets, or objects considered magnetic, that were used by the nineteenth-century mesmerists and Animal Magnetizers. These "magnets" and "tractors" often were purchased by patients who wanted to avoid paying the high fees of their physicians. Experiments by Charcot and others on the induction of a sleeplike state by means of Animal Magnetism ultimately led to the development of hypnotism and to its use in the treatment of some mental disorders. Charcot invented a simple device to be used as a self-hypnotizer by the patient himself.

Gauthier's review of Animal Magnetism (7) presents a much broader view of the subject than was held by other authors. It includes in its definition of magnetism all nonmedicinal and nonsurgical treatments, including massage, hypnotism, and suggestion. Gauthier presented an imposing mass of information on the practice of what he considered to be forms of Animal Magnetism in ancient Egypt, Persia, Greece, Gaul, Rome, and India and in medieval and later Europe.

Today suggestion is not used deliberately and systematically in psychiatric treatment. If anything, the prevailing belief today is that suggestion must be ruled out if real improvement is to occur and persist. However, the idea that the apparent success of some treatment might be due solely to suggestion is by no means new, as shown by Reid (9):

A new medicine will frequently obtain a fortuitous fame, during the continuance of which there is no doubt that it actually produces some of those salutary effects which are ascribed to it. But the fault of these new remedies is that they will not *keep.* For so soon as the caprice of the day has gone by, and fashion has withdrawn its protecting influence, the once celebrated recipe is divested of its beneficial properties, if it become not deleterious; by which it would appear that its reputation had not been the result of its salutary efficacy, but that its salutary efficacy had been, in a great measure at least, the result of its reputation.

Dream Interpretation

Using dreams to learn about unconscious thoughts is, as stated earlier, an ancient practice. It is mentioned in the writings of every era, and it received close attention in nineteenth-century psychiatry. Maudsley (10) said: "Let any one take careful note of his dreams, and he will find that many of the seemingly unfamiliar things with which his mind is then occupied, and which appear to be new and strange productions, are traceable to the unconscious appropriations of the day." He added that an unconscious want may "attain to a knowledge of its aim, and the sort of satisfaction, in dreams before it does so in real life"—a comment that echoed similar statements by earlier authors. Moore (11) wrote in 1845: "How often do we remember having recognized in our dreams those feelings and circumstances which had been lost to our waking consciousness?" And, also in 1845, Griesinger (12) said: "We often observe at such times that the ideas suppressed during waking hours come forth strongly in dreams. To the individual who is distressed by bodily and mental troubles, the dream realizes what reality has refused." He made the startling observation that the imaginary realization of wishes, the denial of which may have caused a psychosis, constitutes most of the subject matter of delusions and

Wilhelm Griesinger, one of the greatest clinicians of the modern era. In 1845 he wrote the clinical psychiatric text that became the definitive work on ego-psychiatry and was plagiarized (without attribution) by many others. He wrote pioneering articles on pericarditis, on mastoiditis, on hookworm anemia (called Griesinger's anemia), on brain injury as a cause of psychomotor epilepsy, and on other subjects. He became professor of medicine at Berlin but died in his prime.

hallucinations, which actually are based on "repressed contending ideas."

Von Feuchtersleben (12) wrote in 1845 that ideas in dreams are determined by the laws of association, and that "dormant ideas," "obscure ideas," and "sensations with dormant consciousness" make up the content of dreams: "in sleep 'the Old Adam' appears." These unconscious thoughts, he said, are also the substance of psychosis; indeed, mental disease is a relapse into a state of dreaming while awake. (This statement repeats similar comments made by others hundreds of years earlier.) He strongly recommended that dreams should be used in psychiatry. He added, however, that the dreams might have to be interpreted:

Dreaming, as the precursor and accompaniment of diseases, deserves continued investigation, not because it is to be considered as a spiritual divination, but because, as the unconscious language of the coenaesthesis and of the *sensorium commune*, it often clearly shows to those who can comprehend its meaning, the state of the patient, though he himself is not aware of this; and the interpretation of dreams deserves the attention and study of the physician, if not any one else.

Charma (14) commented on the extraordinary rapidity of thought in dreams, and concluded that dreams were manifestations of the association of ideas. Johannes Volkelt (15) wrote a book on the interpretation of dreams that was highly praised by Freud.

There are many systematic treatises on dreams (16). Aristotle said that some dreams were true and some false, but he gave no clear method of recognizing each. Cardan resolved this difficulty when he stated that *all* dreams represent repressed appetites, desires, and intentions, a notion that became a cornerstone of psychoanalysis in the twentieth century. (Cardan [17] had some interesting dreams of his own, one of which led to his making a disastrous marriage.)

Logotherapy

The earliest discussions of the power of the word are to be found in the writings of Plato. Before that there are casual references to directing encouraging remarks toward patients, but these can hardly be taken to indicate a serious concern with logotherapy. The Platonic writings deal more with the general problem of persuasion by means of rhetoric, but, as Laín Entralgo (4) shows, some of them applied to psychiatric problems. However, to Plato and those who followed him, logotherapy meant merely the treatment of despondency and of mild to moderate grief reactions. Evidently no attempt was made to treat thinking disorders. The clearest expression has come to us from the Attic poet Antiphon (or perhaps some other person of the same name) (18):

But while he was still busy with poetry he invented a method for curing distress, just as physicians have a treatment for those who are ill; and at Corinth, fitting up a room near the market-place, he wrote on the door that he could cure by words those who were in distress; and by asking questions and finding out the causes of their condition he consoled those in trouble. But thinking this art was unworthy of him he turned to oratory.

However, logotherapy had a more ancient history than that. For example, *The Yellow Emperor's Classic of Internal Medicine* (19) said that "feelings and desires should be investigated and made known" in order to achieve the state of unity that represented "the utmost in the art of healing." Burton (20) reviewed a host of ancient, medieval, and renaissance writings along the same lines. In the nineteenth century logotherapy was firmly established and indeed very popular. For example, Kant's *The Power of the Mind, Through Simple Determination, to Become Master Over Morbid Ideas* (21), first published in 1798, went through several editions in the succeeding half century.* Many writers mentioned some form of logotherapy in passing, as if it were too familiar to require extended discussion. Pinel (22), for example, believed that insanity could be cured "by mildness of treatment and attention to the state of the mind exclusively." He emphasized "the value of consolatory language, kind

---

*Kant's essay was popular in the nineteenth century, and many later authors used titles similar to his. John Barlow wrote "a small book on a great subject" entitled *On Man's Power Over Himself to Prevent or Control Insanity* (1843), and titles of this kind have been used for a large number of twentieth-century American books and articles.

treatment, and the revival of extinguished hopes." Similarly, others mentioned such methods as "psychische Behandlung," "traitement moral," and "psychological treatment." Not all agreed, however. Dendy (23) wrote, "There is an error among the mere metaphysicians that is fraught with extreme danger— the abstract notion of *moral* cause being the chief excitement of mania." He described those who recommended the exclusive use of psychological methods as "hoodwinked by false metaphysics."

Several authors of the time recommended sympathy with the patient's delusions or hallucinations. Reid (9) said:

To command, or to advise a person laboring under nervous depression to be cheerful and alert, is no less idle and absurd, than it would be to command or advise a person under the direct and most intense of the sun's rays to shiver. . . . The practice of laughing at, or scolding a patient of this class is equally cruel and ineffectual. . . . By indirect and imperceptible means, the attention may, in many instances, be gently and insensibly enticed, but seldom can one with safety *force* it from any habitual topic of painful contemplation.

Georget, had this to say (24):

Never combat directly [patients'] unreasonable ideas by discussion, opposition, contradiction, joking or sarcasm. Do not inhibit their ideas, which are necessary to the illness, any more than you would forbid a person with bronchial catarrh to cough.

Spurzheim (25) wrote in a similar vein:

On the whole, the less notice that can be taken even of the most obstinate fancies of the insane, the less disposed will they be to retain them. So fully satisfied am I of this, that I never think of diverting them from their credulity. On the contrary, I make it a rule rather to coincide with their greatest extravagances.

All these ideas are largely extensions of the very ancient belief that it is sometimes wise to accept the patients' delusions. Thessalus of Tralles, for example, and Ambroise Paré, fifteen hundred years later, are reported to have treated patients who had delusions of having swallowed animals by making them vomit into receptacles in which such animals had been surreptitiously placed and then showing the vomitus to the patients.

Von Feuchtersleben's book (13) is an early attempt at a systematic discussion of the principles that underlie logotherapy. His approach is indicated in some scattered comments, for example, "Psychical powers ... may also be used in many cases for the purposes of cure," which requires that the patient develop complete "self-knowledge and self-control," but "who in the full possession of health can boast of having attained this?" In particular he discussed the role of the physician in logotherapy, the aim of which is to reeducate the patient's social feelings and restore the old (healthy) personality. He believed that the physician who is at the same time "physician, remedy, and vehicle" must be

just, equitable, and above all, perfectly dispassionate. . . . We act according to the laws of association; that is to say, we seek to place before the patient those ideas to which we wish to assign, as it were, a larger space in the mind, and desire to render permanent, and which we wish to oppose, in frequent and often repeated connexion to those ideas which are morbid.

Bonn Ernst von Feuchtersleben, dean of the medical school at Vienna (as well as councillor to Emperor Francis Joseph), who wrote perceptively on psychiatric problems and was notable for his extensive discussions of regimen and psychotherapy.

The desirable ideas must be related to an object or to a feeling in order to be made lasting. Bad ideas must be ignored; no attempt should be made to contradict them. Von Feuchtersleben felt that a Socratic technique should be used, since

no truth is so salutary as that which the lunatic suggests to himself. Persuasion from others rather strengthens the patient in the sophistry of error. . . . Above all things, the physician must be furnished with a perfect anamnesis. It is not only necessary to the diagnosis, but is serviceable likewise for the treatment, because this must be guided by a knowledge of the patient's personality.

The application of the psychical mode of cure is particularly difficult. Supposing us, notwithstanding the above-mentioned obstacles, to have obtained a thorough insight into the character, the peculiarities, and the actual state of a lunatic patient, we are nevertheless still in want of a comparative standard by which we might accurately determine the degree of every affection which we intend to employ as a remedy, so that this mode of treatment becomes very uncertain, and, from the delicate operation of such mental influences, we may do as much harm, as we mean to do good. . . . We do not know how many grains of pleasure are necessary for a melancholy patient, that he may be cheered and not made still more sullen. In no department of medicine is it more necessary to individualise; while in none is this left so entirely to the tact of the physician as in the treatment of mental diseases.

The physician must recognize "a too great readiness of the patient to conform to the wishes of the physician" and "a certain uniformity of expression, which indicates phrases learned by rote without having any meaning attached to them."

Winslow's comments (26) were more profound and perceptive than those of others:

The practitioner of medicine forms but a low and grovelling estimate of his high destination, and the duties of his dignified vocation, if he conceives that his operations are limited to a successful application of mere physical agents. The physician is daily called upon in the exercise of his profession to witness the powerful effect of mental emotion upon the material fabric. He reognizes the fact although he may be unable to explain its rationale.

In proportion as the physician estimates the effect of moral causes of disease, will he be a successful practitioner, elevate himself in the social scale, and not only deserve, but command, the respect of the public, and place the science of medicine upon the highest vantage ground of which it is susceptible. How is it possible for the practitioner to influence the minds of others, if he has no knowledge of the laws governing his own understanding? As well might he administer for the relief of an acute malady, a material agent of whose properties and *modus operandi* he is avowedly ignorant.

Maudsley (10) also made systematic comments on logotherapy. Among other things, he stressed the need for a detailed consideration "of the circumstances in which [the patient] has lived, and in relation to which he has developed, as well as the observation of his habits of thought, feeling and action." He also remarked on the difficulties of determining the causes of the disease:

The causes of insanity, as usually enumerated by authors, are so general and vague as to render it a very difficult matter to settle in the mind what they really are. But it is hardly less difficult, when brought face to face with an actual case of insanity, and when there is every opportunity of investigation, to determine with certainty what have been the causes of the disease. The uncertainty springs from the fact that, in the great majority of cases, there is a concurrence of conditions, not one single effective cause. All the conditions which conspire to the production of an

Henry Maudsley, who with Griesinger and Janet, was one of the greatest psychiatrists of all time.

effect are alike causes, alike agents; and, therefore, all the conditions, whether they are in the individual or in the circumstances in which he is placed, which in a given case co-operate in the production of disease, must alike be regarded as causes. When we are told that a man has become deranged from anxiety or grief, we have learned very little if we rest content with that. How does it happen that another man, subjected to an exactly similar cause of grief, does not go mad? It is certain that the entire causes cannot be the same where the effects are so different; and what we want to have laid bare is the conspiracy of conditions, internal and external, by which a mental shock, inoperative in one case, has had such serious consequences in another. A complete biograhpical account of the individual, not neglecting the consideration of his hereditary antecedents, would alone suffice to set forth distinctly the causation of his insanity. If all the circumstances, internal and external, were duly scanned and weighed, it would be found that there is no accident in madness; the disease, whatever form it might take, by whatsoever complex concurrence of conditions, or by how many successive links of causation, it might be generated, would be traceable as the inevitable consequence of certain antecedents, as plainly as the explosion of gunpowder may be traced to its causes, whether the train of events of which it is the issue be long or short. The germs of insanity are sometimes latent in the foundations of the character, and the final outbreak is perhaps the explosion of a long train of antecedent preparations (pp. 197-198).*

Many authors, among them Esquirol, Guislain, Georget, and Voisin, recognizing that the disorders discussed here were as likely to have physical causes as emotional ones, nevertheless recommended logotherapy. Of course, logotherapy depended to a considerable degree on the physician's ability to communicate with the patient.† Methods of obtaining data from persons unwilling to talk at all have been considered for centuries. The medieval approach was dramatic but probably not effective. According to the great thirteenth-century encyclopedia compiled by Dominican monks under Vincent of Beauvais, an owl's heart

*The use of the anamnesis in psychologic investigation was not an innovation of nineteenth-century physicians. The anamnesis was believed to have been used for that purpose by the Lord of Darkness for many centuries previously. Before seducing a victim, Satan was apparently accustomed to studying his intended victim's mental and physical status, his social and health history, his temperament, etc., in order to determine how best to lead the victim perhaps to ruin here on earth and certainly to eternal damnation. (See More, T., *Utopia and a Dialogue of Comfort Against Tribulation*. L. Miles, ed. Bloomington: Indiana University Press, 1965, p. 118.)

†Séglas held that *all* the words of psychotic patients were significant. (See Séglas, J. *Les troubles du langage chez les aliénés*. Paris: Alcan, 1892.)

placed on the left side of a sleeping woman would make her tell everything she had done. The *Experimenta Alberti* of Albertus Magnus extended the range of usefulness of the procedure. It stated that if the owl's heart and right foot were placed on a sleeper, he would immediately tell whatever he had done and would answer any questions asked of him. Nineteenth-century psychiatrists were completely baffled by the problem of the unwilling patient, and consequently psychotherapy could not be applied in such instances. The number of these cases was reduced somewhat in the twentieth century by the use of the sodium amytal interview.

A technique used to elicit unconscious thoughts was needed. Free association was suggested for this purpose. (It had been used as a literary device in the past, notably in the late eighteenth century by Schiller, the German poet—who also was a physician.) Many writers questioned the validity of any data on unconscious thinking that could be obtained through introspection. For example, Broussais (27) wrote:

They say that we must listen to the language of consciousness; and for

F. J. V. Broussais, who derogated free association and was skeptical about our ability to know the unconscious mind. A privateersman, seargent in Napolean's army, he became a professor of medicine at Paris and head of Les Invalides, *the veteran's administration of the post-Napoleonic period.*

that purpose collect ourselves in silence and obscurity, that no sense may
be employed; we must abstract ourselves from everybody in nature, in
short we must listen to ourselves alone, and think. . . . It will be impossible
to assert, after this inspection of the interior, a single fact that will not
require to be verified by the senses.

And Von Feuchtersleben (13) added that we acquire psychologic
knowledge

by an accurate investigation of what passes within ourselves, But how few
men are capable of taking such a view of themselves as is neither
prejudiced nor hypochondriacally exaggerated, nor superficial? . . . We do
not observe the springs of our psychical functions when they are in active
operation, but only when they are quiescent and cannot be investigated (p.
20).

Maudsley, on the one hand, believed that "in the deepest
and most secret recesses of the mind, there is nothing hidden
from the individual self, or from others, which may not be thus
some time accidentally revealed," but he also held that "the
preconscious action of the mind, as certain metaphysical
psychologists in Germany have called it, and the unconscious
action of the mind, which is now established beyond all rational
doubt, are assuredly facts of which the most ardent psychologist
must admit that self-consciousness can give no account." He
added a critical comment (10):

A positive tendency, which no one can avoid, to interpret the action
of another mind according to the measure of one's own, to see not what is
in the object, but what is in the subject, frequently vitiates an assured
penetration into motives. . . . [The value of introspection as a science] must
plainly rest upon the sufficiency and reliability of consciousness as a
witness of that which takes place in the mind. Is the foundation then
sufficiently secure? It may well be doubted; and for the following reasons:
    (a) There are but few individuals who are capable of attending to the
succession of phenomena in their own minds; such introspection demanding
a particular cultivation, and being practised with success by those only who
have learned the terms, and been imbued with the theories, of the system
of psychology supposed to be thereby established.
    (b) There is no agreement between those who have acquired the power
of introspection: and men of apparently equal cultivation and capacity will,
with the utmost sincerity and confidence, lay down directly contradictory
propositions. It is not possible to convince either opponnent of error, as it

might be in a matter of objective science, because he appeals to a witness whose evidence can be taken by no one but himself, but whose veracity, therefore, cannot be tested.

(c) To direct consciousness inwardly to the observation of a particular state of mind is to isolate that activity for the time, to cut it off from its relations, and, therefore, to render it unnatural. In order to observe its own action, it is necessary that the mind pause from activity; and yet it is the train of activity that is to be observed. As long as you cannot effect the pause necessary for self-contemplation, there can be no observation of the current of activity: if the pause is effected, then there can be nothing to observe. This cannot be accounted a vain and theoretical objection; for the results of introspection too surely confirm its validity: what was a question once is a question still, and instead of being resolved by introspective analysis is only fixed and fed.

(d) The madman's delusion is of itself sufficient to excite profound distrust, not only in the objective truth, but in the subjective worth of the testimony of an individual's self-consciousness. Descartes laid it down as the fundamental proposition of philosophy that whatever the mind could clearly and distinctly conceive, was true: if there is one thing more clearly and distinctly conceived than another, it is commonly the madman's delusion. No marvel, then, that psychologists, since the time of Descartes, have held that the veracity of consciousness is to be relied upon only under certain rules, from the violation of which, Sir W. Hamilton believed, the contradictions of philosophy have arisen. On what evidence then do the rules rest? Either on the evidence of consciousness, whence it happens that each philosopher and each lunatic has his own rules, and no advance is made; or upon the observation and judgment of mankind, to confess which is very much like throwing self-consciousness overboard—not otherwise than as was advantageously done by positive science when the figures on the thermometer, and not the subjective feelings of heat or cold, were recognized to be the true test of the individual's temperature.

It is not merely a charge against self-consciousness that it is not reliable in that of which it does give information; but it is a provable charge against it that it does not give any account of a large and important part of our mental activity: its light reaches only to states of consciousness, and not to states of mind. Its evidence then is not only untrustworthy save under conditions which it nowise helps us to fix, but it is of little value, because it has reference only to a small part of that for which its testimony is invoked. May we not then justly say that self-consciousness is utterly incompetent to supply the facts for the building up of a truly inductive psychology? ... How then was it possible that a one-sided method, which entirely ignored the examination of nature, should do more than repeat the same things over and over again in words which, though they might be different, were yet not less indefinite? The results have answered to the absurdity of the method: for, after being in fashion for more than two thousand years, nothing has been established by it (pp. 4–15).

Probably, the most influential of all the writings on free association was that of Galton, in 1879 (28). (Freud translated this paper into German for the use of physicians and medical students.) Galton wrote:

It remains to summarise what has been said in the foregoing memoir. I have desired to show how whole strata of mental operations that have lapsed out of ordinary consciousness, admit of being dragged into light, recorded and treated statistically, and how the obscurity that attends the initial steps of our thoughts can thus be pierced and dissipated. I then showed measurably the rate at which associations sprung up, their character, the date of their first formation, their tendency to recurrence, and their relative precedence. Also I gave an instance showing how the phenomenon of a long-forgotten scene, suddenly starting into consciousness, admitted in many cases of being explained. Perhaps the strongest of the impressions left by these experiments regards the multifariousness of the work done by the mind in a state of half-unconsciousness, and the valid reason they afford for believing in the existence of still deeper strata of mental operations, sunk wholly below the level of consciousness, which may account for such mental phenomena as cannot otherwise be explained. We gain an insight by these experiments into the marvellous number and nimbleness of our mental associations, and we also learn that they are very

Francis Galton, whose writings on anthopologic subjects were outstanding. He introduced, indirectly, free-association into psychologic studies.

far indeed from being infinite in their variety. We find that our working stock of ideas is narrowly limited, but that the mind continually recurs to them in conducting its operations, therefore its tracks necessarily become more defined and its flexibility diminished as age advances.

MILIEU THERAPY

Kindness in the treatment of mental disease came to replace force as a result of the Enlightenment. In the first place, the belief that demoniacal possession was the cause of mental disease was rejected by the intelligent. Second, preoccupation with the rights of man came to the force. Both these factors stimulated interest in a new approach to the treatment of the insane. A number of laymen had already proposed this approach, for example, St. Vincent de Paul (who, among other good works, raised money for the Bicêtre and the Salpêtrière). Although Pinel, among physicians, has long been given the credit for inventing milieu therapy, his remarks on the subject were unimpressively brief and general.* Pinel stated that "insanity could be cured by mildness of treatment and attention to the state of the mind exclusively," that coercion might be "very effectively applied without corporeal indignity," and that one should recognize "the value of consolatory language, kind treatment, and the revival of extinguished hopes." Members of the Society of Friends, notably the Tukes at the York Retreat, probably had much more influence in this regard, both in their own work and through their followers, of whom Conolly was the most famous. He wrote two books, one of which (29) discussed general principles the other (30) summarized his decades of using milieu therapy. In the first book he decried the

---

*The popular notion that Pinel was the innovator of humane treatment in psychiatry has wide currency today, but it receives little support from any academic or professional quarter. In the first place, although he did free the patients from their chains at the Bicêtre in 1792, in many cases it was only to place them in some other form of restraint, as his *Treatise* (22) shows. What is more important, however, is that the patients had been freed from their chains in Italy in 1788, before Pinel's *Treatise* was written. The movement to free the patients from their changes was fully developed, although the practice was by no means universal, in England in the early 1780s. This matter is fully discussed in Grange, K. M. "Pinel or Chiarugi?" *Medical History* 7:371–380, 1963.

*J. Connolly, head of the York
Retreat, an ardent propagan-
dist for milieu therapy, highly
popular in America in the mid-
nineteenth century and again,
as a new discovery, for a time
in the mid-twentieth.*

haste of some physicians to incarcerate patients in order to get
"rid of [their own] anxiety and the patient together" (29). He
went on:

> But by far the most lamentable part of the present system of lunatic
> houses is, that a residence in them is detrimental in exact proportion to the
> favourable nature of the case. . . . The crowd of most of our asylums is
> made up of odd but harmless individuals, not much more absurd than
> numbers who are at large. When eccentric habits are growing upon a man
> who continues to mix in society, they may be checked by his own efforts,
> on observing the surprise or the amusement which is caused by them. The
> starts of irritability, and the gloom of discontent, are alike corrected by
> prudential feelings, or by regard for others, or by the continual interrup-
> tions of business or pleasure. In an asylum for lunatics, the eccentric man
> makes little or no effort to correct his eccentricity; nor the irritable man
> his irritability; and the man of gloom sits in motionless despondency from
> morning until night, without salutary disturbance of duty, or necessary
> exertion, or the visit of a cheerful friend. To all these patients,
> confinement is the very reverse of beneficial. It fixes and renders
> permanent what might have passed away, and ripens eccentricity, or
> temporary excitement or depression, into actual insanity;—and this is not

the worst part of the evil; for even when a patient has suffered no aggravation of his disorder during its greatest severity, the danger is not passed: nay, it is increased as his convalescence advances; for when that otherwise happy change commences, the sights and sounds of a lunatic asylum become, if they were not before, both afflicting and unsalutary. That, during the unconfirmed stage of convalescence, when reason is struggling through the cloud which has obscured it, some mental as well as medical treatment is required, is, I presume, what no man will deny, who has really ever thought upon the subject. But can it be applied—is it possible that it should be applied—in the generality of cases in our lunatic asylums? A slight recollection of the circumstances in which a lunatic is placed, will furnish a ready answer to the question (pp. 16–18).[*]

In his second book (30) Conolly described with remarkable self-satisfaction the effects of changes he made at the Middlesex Lunatic Asylum at Hanwell. He listed such topics as "disuse of mechanical restraints," "the number of attendants increased," "vigilance and moral management substituted for restraint," "want of resources in offices and attendants accustomed to rely upon restraint," "necessity of forbearance in the management of lunatics," "no mechanical restraint resorted to for ten years," "reception and treatment of a newly admitted patient," "occupations, etc., in the day time," "evening entertainments," and "necessity of having kind and conscientious attendants." Over fifty pages of text were used to describe the spread of his ideas to other English hospitals. In this book (30), Conolly stated:

In all asylums the statistical registers show that the recoveries, in the recent cases admitted, are in the first year numerous; that in the second year from the commencement of the malady they are much fewer; and that in the third and subsequent years they become rare. ... [In good hospitals] one-half, perhaps two-thirds of the recent cases recover; whilst not one-third, perhaps not one-fourth, of those recover who are injudiciously treated on the first appearance of the malady. ... The use of whirling-chairs, baths of surprise, violent effusions over the body, prolonged immersion in water, and all similar devices, are universally condemned.

___

[*]Conolly (29) made the remarkable comment that kindly treatment was applied only with difficulty to young people from the city (p. 126) and to liberated women (p. 127). He recommended (p. 162) that the education of the young accord with Combe's phrenologic writings and also with the principles of Barlow's Man's Power Over Himself to Prevent or Control Insanity (London: Pickering, n.d.). Not the least interesting of Conolly's use of water in treatment was his reference to the waterbed (p. 170).

Much of what Conolly said resembles statements by today's proponents of milieu therapy. Conolly is modern not only in his views about how to use milieu therapy but also in proclaiming, without relying on data, its superiority over all other forms of treatment. As might be expected, Conolly sneered at shock therapy and emphasized patients' untoward reactions to it.

Although Conolly's views were not universally accepted, many influential European physicians, notably in France, adopted his methods, for example, François Leuret (31).

Maudsley's discussion (10) of milieu therapy, was, as would be expected, both scholarly and progressive. He wrote:

Let it be clearly understood that I am not now advocating the placing of an insane patient alone in a cottage with one or two attendants; in such case I readily admit that he is subjected to the most odious kind of tyranny, and to a deprivation of liberty in its worst form—that he would be a thousand times better off in a well-conducted asylum, and certainly could not be worse off in the worst asylum. I am arguing distinctly in favour of placing certain chronic insane persons in private families, where after a time they become truly a part of the family, and are considered in all its arrangements, not otherwise than as a member of it afflicted with some incurable bodily disease would be. In such case the loss of liberty is by no means equal to that in an asylum, where the occasional indulgences of a certain freedom granted only serve to lighten up the present misery and to deepen the gloom of the outlook into the future. . . .

. . . In the village of Hanwell, and its nieghbourhood, there are several single patients living with private families, some Chancery patients, and others not, who are extremely well taken care of in every regard; what insurmountable impediment is there to that which is done successfully in Hanwell being done in any other village in England? It would be difficult to assign any such. . . . When official views and practice have been modified and brought into conformity with the stream of liberal thought, as we cannot doubt that they surely will be, and when arrangements have been made for a systematic and more frequent visitation of single patients, then it cannot be doubted that the number of these will rapidly increase, to their infinite comfort, to the pressingly needed relief of our overgrown and over-crowded asylums, and to the general advantage of the community.

For the reasons adduced, I cannot but think that future progress in the improvement of the treatment of the insane lies in the direction of lessening the sequestration and increasing the liberty of them. Many chronic insane, incurable and harmless, will be allowed to spend the remaining days of their sorrowful pilgrimage in private families, having the comforts of family life, and the priceless blessing of the utmost freedom that is compatible with their proper care. The one great impediment to this reform at present undoubtedly lies in the public ignorance, the unreasoning fear, and the selfish avoidance of insanity. . . .

Moral Treatment. To remove the patient from the midst of those circumstances under which insanity has been produced must be the first aim of treatment. There is always extreme difficulty in treating satisfactorily an insane person in his own house amongst his own kindred, where he has been accustomed to exercise authority, or to exact attention, and where he continually finds new occasions for outbreaks of anger or fresh food for his delusions. An entire change in the surroundings will sometimes of itself lead to his recovery. . . .

The patient having been removed from those influences which have conspired to the production of the disease, and now tend to keep it up, and having been made to recognise from without a control which he cannot exercise from within, it remains to strive patiently and persistently by every inducement to arouse him from his self-brooding or self-exaltation, and to engage his attention in matters external—to make him step out of himself. This is best done by interesting him in some occupation, or in a variety of amusements; and it will be done the more easily now that the surroundings have been entirely changed. The activity of the morbid thoughts and feelings subsiding in new relations and under new impressions, more healthy feelings may be gradually awakened; and the activity of healthy thought and feeling will not fail in its turn further to favour the decay of morbid feeling. If there is some fixed delusion, it will do no good to enter upon any systematic argument against it; there would be almost as much hope of an argument against the east wind or against a convulsion; but by engaging the mind in other thoughts as much as possible, and thus substituting a healthy energy for the morbid energy, the force of the delusion will be most likely to abate, and finally to die out. But; although it is of no avail to talk against a delusion, it is important to avoid assenting to it: by quiet dissent or a mild expression of incredulity when it is mentioned, the patient should be made to understand clearly that he is in a minority of one, and that, though a person in a minority of one may perchance be a genius in advance of the rest of mankind, it is infintely more likely that he is a madman far behind it (pp. 428–434).

Milieu therapy, when used in the nineteenth century, failed to produce the results promised, and was soon abandoned, only to be revived enthusiastically, in America during the wave of do-goodism that swept the country in the mid-twentieth century.

SHOCK THERAPIES

The origin of shock therapies for mental disease can only be conjectured. As stated earlier, one basis of the treatment was clearly to persuade an invading demon that it would be more comfortable elsewhere. Another basis was offered by the ancient dogma called metasyncrisis, or in modern terms, the omelette theory. This holds that a patient's organism must be thoroughly disrupted in order that it might be reconstituted into a more desirable state. (Thessalus of Tralles, a physician of Nero's time, is usually credited with the formulation of this concept, but this attribution is of dubious validity.) This hypothesis still exists in psychiatric treatment. For example, a few years ago so-called regressive shock therapy was used; the patient received treatments several times a day until he was reduced to a state of (temporary) imbecility, after which the patient was reformed by the psychiatrist, presumably in the psychiatrist's own image.

Several physicians of the ancient and medieval eras recommended the use of a swinging chair to initiate metasyncrisis. There is no way of knowing why the swinging chair was given this power. One possibility that I suggested some time ago was that since medicine, like religion, thrived on syncretism, the origin of the swinging chair notion might be found in the ancient Attic practice of swinging small images from trees to prevent or cure madness in women. This practice was said to have originated after one of the many waves of suicide by hanging that attended the introduction of the Dionysian religion into southern Greece.* Perhaps in later years some literal-minded physician transferred the swinging from the image to the patient.

Around 1800 Erasmus Darwin reported that he had found lying on a revolving millstone soothing to the point of slumber (32). That anyone could be lulled to sleep by lying amid the grinding vibrations of the stone, together with the banging and whirring noises of the rest of the machinery, plus the roar of the water in the race was undoubtedly a source of wonder. At any rate within a few years patients were being centrifuged in mental hospitals (33). A variety of centrifuges, sometimes comprising

---

*One legend states that Icarius, having received the vine from Dionysus, introduced it into Greece. The first men he gave wine to fell down in a stupor; their friends thought Icarius had poisoned them and thereupon killed him. His daughter found the corpse and hanged herself. Dionysus punished the land with a plague and an epidemic of insanity that affected the maidens, so that they hanged themselves. To avert a return of the curse, the Festival of the Swing was inaugurated: small images were hung from trees and swung on the appointed day each year.

swinging chairs, came into use.[*] Although physicians such as Cox, Knight, Hallaran, and Prichard recommended this treatment, others denounced it. Steward (2) wrote:

It is a remedy which would be tolerated in no disease but insanity. Unless tried, it is quite impossible to conceive the suffering produced by it. The author speaks confidently from having himself tried it (pp. 56–57).

Conolly (30) used equally strong words:

The horizontal position [was] adopted when the object was to procure sleep; and the erect posture, the other failing in cases of excitement, to procure intestinal action. It is acknowledged that patients subjected to the swing were ever after terrified at the mention of it; that it lowered the pulse and the temperature to such a degree as to alarm the physician; that it occasioned a disagreeable suffusion of the countenance; frequently leaving an ecchymosis of the eyes; that it acted as an emetic, and as a hypercathartic; but it still was lauded as reducing the unmanageable, and, stranger still, as causing the melancholy to take "a natural interest in the affairs of life" (p. 14).

Another form of shock therapy was the "surprise bath." Since immersing the body in water was held, by both physicians and laymen, to be highly hazardous, this was a particularly terrifying form of treatment. In practice, the patient was either doused with water or dropped or thrown into it.[†] The patients were cleaner, if not saner, after this treatment. On the other hand, sedative baths were recommended by many physicians.

[*]See, for example, Horn in *Zeitschrift für Psychische, Ärzte*, 1818, p. 219, describing *da Drehbett or die Drehmaschine* then in use in Berlin. Other centrifuges are pictured in Altschule, M. D. *The Roots of Modern Psychiatry*. 2nd ed. New York: Grune and Stratton. 1965, pp. 147–150.

[†]Some devices used are pictured in Altschule, M. D. loc. cit., pp. 144, 145.

In 1806 total submersion for three or four minutes in the Connecticut River was tried on a deranged person, the Honorable Richard Whitney, of Hinsdale, New Hampshire, in the hope that "this desperate ordeal . . . would divert his mind, break the chain of unhappy associations, and thus remove the cause of his disease. Upon trial, this system of regeneration proved of no avail, for with the returning consciousness of the patient came the knell of departed hopes, as he exclaimed " 'You can't drown love.' "

A short time later Dauerschlaff was induced with opium, and this was fatal. These events led one of Whitney's neighbors to endow the establishment of the Brattleboro Retreat. (See Draper, J. *The Vermont Asylum for the Insane, Its annals for Fifty Years*. Brattleboro, Vt.: Hildreth and Fales, 1887, p. 7.)

Electricity came into the picture soon after its use in medicine began. Thus in 1747 Bianchini (34) mentioned the application of electricity to parts of the body. Desbois de Rochefort's great classic (35) on treatment (published post-humously in 1779) summarizes eighteenth-century ideas about the uses of electricity. In this book, the use of electricity in non-organic nervous diseases is recommended, and its success with a patient suffering from a grief reaction is cited. Its use in psychoses is also described. The techniques included "commotions électriques," in which electricity was applied in succession to the vertex, occiput, neck, spinal column, and kidneys. The book warned of the dangerous excitement that might follow the application of electricity to the head. Galvanism waxed and waned in popularity for a century thereafter. Hill (36) recommended it for depressions. This form of psychiatric therapy has only historical interest at present, since its use caused no measurable improvement. Nevertheless, since it afforded much important information on neuromuscular function, it did bring about a better understanding of some neurologic disorders. It also may have had a profound effect on the course of psychiatry; when Freud, then working in Erb's clinic, saw that it was ineffective, he turned to psychological methods.

An interesting sidelight involves the discovery of electrically induced convulsions. The discovery of the beneficial effect of convulsions induced by metrazol in the treatment of depressions is now generally recognized as one of the most important events of modern psychiatry. However, it was not until electricity came to be used to induce the convulsions that shock treatment became simple and safe enough to encourage its widespread use. Nevertheless, it is not generally recognized that in 1871 a well-known American physician, G. M. Beard, clearly described the induction of convulsions by applying electric currents to the head. Beard and Rockwell (37) published their book in 1871. Its nearly 700 pages included, among other things, a meticulously detailed account of the indications for and techniques of electrotherapy. The application of electricity to the head was recommended for the treatment of what would now be called neurotic, hypochondriacal, and hysterical complaints. An electrode was to be placed on each temple, over each ear, or on each of the mastoid processes, or one electrode was placed on the forehead and a second on the occiput. The authors stated that prolonged treatment might cause convulsions, which they regarded as an undesirable effect. Nevertheless, they clearly called attention to the induction of seizures by the cranial application of electricity almost three-quarters of a century before Cerletti rediscovered the method.

COMMENT

The early history of the treatment of psychiatric patients by physicians shows that there has been no change in approach and surprisingly little change in techniques, at least until the development of chemotherapy. This dependence on the past is, in this age of purported scorn for tradition, simultaneously reassuring and discouraging. However we may react to the situation today, we must accustom ourselves to a feeling of *déjà vu*. The controversies of a century or two ago are the controversies of today.

REFERENCES

1. Marx, O. M. Diet in European psychiatric hospitals, jails, and general hospitals in the first half of the 19th century according to travellers' reports. *Journal of the History of Medicine* 217, 1968.
2. Steward, J. B. *Practical notes on insanity*. London: J. Churchill, 1845.
3. Stephen-Chauvet. *La médicine chez les peuples primitives*. Paris: Librairie Maloine, 1936.
   Roney, J. G. The occurrence of trephining among the Bakhtiari. *Bulletin of the History of Medicine* 28:489, 1954.
4. Laín Entralgo, P. *The therapy of the word in classical antiquity*. L. J. Rather and J. M. Sharp, trans. New Haven, Conn.: Yale University Press, 1970.
5. See also Shakespeare's *The Merchant of Venice*, Act IV, Scene 1: "Others, when the bagpipe sings i' the nose, cannot contain their urine."
6. Fodor, N. The poltergeist-psychoanalyzed. *Psychiatric Quarterly* 22:195, 1940.
7. Gauthier, A. *Introduction au magnétisme*. Paris: Dentu, 1840.
8. Pattie, F. A. Mesmer's medical dissertation and its debt to Mead's *De Imperio Solis ac Lunae*. *Journal of the History of Medicine and Allied Sciences* 11:275, 1956.

9. Reid, J. *Essays on hypochondriasis and other nervous affections.* 3rd ed. London: Longman, Hurst, Rees, Orme, and Brown, 1823, p. 343.

10. Maudsley, H. *The psysiology and pathology of the mind.* New York: D. Appleton, 1867.

11. Moore, G. *The power of the mind over the body, considered in relation to health and morals.* New York: Harper and Brothers, 1845.

12. Griesinger, W. *Mental pathology and therapeutics.* C. L. Robertson and J. Rutherford, trans. London: New Sydenham Society, 1867.

13. Von Feuchtersleben, E. *The principles of medical psychology.* H. E. Lloyd, trans. London: Sydenham Society, 1847.

14. Charma, A. *Du sommeil.* Paris: Hachette, 1851.

15. Volkelt, J. *Die Traum-Phantasie.* Stuttgart: Meyer and Zeller, 1875.

16. Ratcliff, A. J. J. *A history of dreams.* Boston: Small, Maynard, 1923.
    Woods, R. L. *The world of dreams: An anthology.* New York: Random House, 1947.
    Devereux, G. *Reality and dream.* New York: International Universities Press, 1951.

17. Cardan, J. *The book of my life.* Trans. from the Latin by J. Stoner. New York: Dutton, 1930, p. 90.

18. Plutarch. *Moralia.* Vol. 10. Loeb Classical Library, Cambridge, Mass., Harvard University Press, n.d., p. 351.

19. *The Yellow Emperor's classic of internal medicine.* I. Veith, trans. Baltimore: Williams and Wilkins, 1949.

20. Burton, R. *The anatomy of melancholy* (1628). Trans. from the 5th (1651) Latin ed. by F. Dell and P. Jordan-Smith. New York: Tudor, 1948.

21. Kant, I. *Von der Macht des Gemuths durch den blossen Vorsatz seiner krankhaften Gefuhle Meister zu Seyn.* Jena: Academischen Buchhandlung, 1798.

22. Pinel, P. *A treatise on insanity, in which are contained the principles of a new and more practical nosology of maniacal disorders.* D. D. Davis, trans. Sheffield: W. Dodd, 1806.

23. Dendy, W. C. *The philosophy of mystery.* New York: Harper and Brothers, n.d. (probably about 1860), p. 106.

24. Georget, M. *De la folie: Considerations sur cette maladie.* Paris: Chez Crevot, 1820.

25. Spurzheim, J. G. *Observations on the deranged manifestations of the mind.* 3rd American ed. Boston: Marsh, Capen, and Lyon, 1836, p. 137.

26. Winslow, F. *Lettsonian lectures on insanity.* London: J. Churchill, 1854, pp. 40–41.

27. Broussais, F. J. V. *On irritation and insanity.* T. Cooper, trans. Columbia, S.C.: S. J. M. Morris, 1831, pp. 85, 87.

28. Galton, F. Psychometric experiments. *Brain* 2:149–162, 1879.

29. Conolly, J. *An inquiry concerning the indications of insanity, with suggestions for the better protection of the insane.* London: John Taylor, 1830.

30. Conolly, J. *The treatment of insanity without mechanical restraint.* London: Smith, Elder, 1856, pp. 68, 279–280.

31. Leuret, F. *Traitement moral de la folie.* Paris: J. B. Ballière, 1840.

32. Darwin, E. *Zoönomia, or laws of organic life.* 2nd ed., from 3rd London ed. Boston: Thomas and Andrews, 1803.

33. Cox, J. M. *Practical observations on insanity.* 3rd ed. London: R. Baldwin and T. Underwood, 1813.
   Hallaran, W. S. *The number of insane and the cure of insanity.* Cork: Edwards and Savage, 1810.
   Knight, P. S. *Derangement of the mind.* London: Longman, Rees, Orme, Brown, and Green, 1827.
   Prichard, J. C. *Treatise on insanity and other disorders affecting the mind.* London: Sherwood, Gilbert, and Piper, 1835.

34. Bianchini, G. F. *Saggio d'esperienze intorno la medicina elettrica fatte in Venezia da Alcuni Amatori di Fisica.* Venice: G. Pasquali, 1749.

35. Desbois de Rochefort. *Cours elémentaire de matière médicale: Ouvrage posthume.* Paris: Méquignon l'Aîné, 1779.

36. Hill, G. N. *An essay on the prevention and cure of insanity.* London: Longman, Hurst, Rees, Orme, and Brown, 1814.

37. Beard, G. M., and Rockwell, A. D. *A practical treatise on the medical and surgical uses of electricity.* New York: W. Wood, 1871.

Chapter 8

ACUPUNCTURE IN THE WESTERN WORLD
up to a century ago

Lithograph by an unknown artist, Paris, c. 1820. The print satirizes the claimed effects of acupuncture. A picture of the patron saint of acupuncture, St. Sebastian, full of arrows on the day of his martyrdom, hangs on the wall.

The origin of acupuncture is so remote in time as to be unknown. It seems to have developed out of a superstitious belief that the body contained Yang and Yin, the two universal principles recognized by ancient Chinese philosophies. Yang was held to mean specifically "sunny side of the hill or river." Yang symbolized sun, heat, fire, heaven, day, dryness, right, light, expansion, upward and outward flow, fertility, manliness, motion, life, highness, nobility, goodness, beauty, virtue, order, reward, joy, wealth, health, maleness, and so forth, in short almost everything good, strong, or desirable. Yin represented all the opposites.

All happenings, qualities, and objects in nature (including people) were regarded as the resultants of pairs of opposites. It was believed that neither absolute Yang nor absolute Yin could exist, but perfect harmony between the two in a person gave health, whereas disharmony caused death. Ancient Chinese anatomists, who had never bothered to carry out dissection, held that the vascular system consists of twelve pairs of main vessels and their branches; these vessels were believed to carry the blood and air to different parts of the body. These imaginary vessels corresponded to some degree to the known arteries, veins, and capillaries, but the correspondence was most superficial, and, in fact, distinctions between the various kinds of vessels were never clearly made.* The theoretical formulation included twelve pairs of ligaments that followed the same course as the vessels.

Although no one had ever seen this vascular system, the authorities described it in detail and made emphatic statements about where the vessels began, ran, and ended. The then current belief was that the conduits that dispersed Yang and Yin were all submerged, surfacing only at 365 points. These 365 points, dispersed along the course of these hypothetical vessels, were all given fanciful names and were designated as the only points to be used for acupuncture. It was believed that the puncturing of these points evacuated hypothetically trapped air from the hypothetical conduits.

In ancient China there were three recognized methods of treatment: acupuncture, moxa, and massage. Acupuncture is said to have been invented by Huang Ti, and in the T'ang dynasty it formed one of the main branches of medicine, a special chair being established with a "professor" in charge of it. However, it was under the Sungs that acupuncture may be said to have started to become a science, for the first monograph on it was published during this period. In 1027 the then reigning Emperor caused two copper models of the human body to be made with markings to illustrate the principles of acupuncture and holes to designate the points for puncturing. Each figure showed the 365 traditional points, and indicated their names and their supposed relations to the hypothetical submerged conduits. One model was placed in the Imperial Academy of Medicine at Peking and the other in the Jin Chi Palace. Each hole for puncturing had a coating of yellow wax on the surface, while the interior of the model was filled with water. The student was required to practice needling the spot where there was a hidden hole.

The practice of acupuncture consisted of placing needles of various sizes and lengths in the approved points. Nine kinds of needles were officially recognized: arrow-headed, blunt,

---

*The remarkable ideas of the distribution of the vital principle in humans adhered to by the Chinese and Japanese were evidently known in Europe. The year 1682 saw the publication of *Specimen Medicinae Sinicae, sive Opuscula Medica ad Mentum Sinensium*, edited by Andreas Cleter (Frankfort: Joannis Petri Zubrodt). Among its many illustrations are several that show Chinese anatomical ideas that underlay acupuncture.

Title page of Andreas Cleter's book on Chinese medicine, 1682.

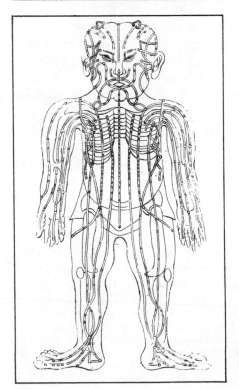

Illustration of the imagined circulatory system of Yang and Yin, from Cleter's book.

156

puncturing, spear-pointed, ensiform, round, capillary, long, and large. They were made of steel, copper, or silver and, in more ancient times, of flint.

In modern practice, the needles are inserted into the flesh, more or less deeply, or may be driven in by a blow with a light mallet. They may be used hot or cold, and occasionally are left *in situ* for days. The patient is usually ordered to cough during the process of insertion. The point of insertion, the direction of the rotation of the needles, the number of needles, the depth of the puncture, and the length of time they are left in—all depend upon the nature and severity of the individual condition. Acupuncture is widely practiced today in east Asia and is there considered a universal panacea. It is used chiefly in treating cholera, colic, cough, rheumatism, sprains, swollen joints, and deep-seated pain of all kinds. An excellent account of the early history of acupuncture in China is presented by Wong and Wu (1).

Moxa, or moxibution, as it is sometimes called, is another method peculiarly Chinese having a very ancient origin. It uses combustible cones of artemisia moxa (common mugwort) applied on the skin at certain spots and then ignited. These cones are placed in a geometrical figure, the sites frequently being the epigastric region, the upper part of the sternum, and the front of the ear. As the smoldering fire burns into the skin, a blister is raised; hence its effect is similar to counter-irritation or cauterization, but more painful. The resulting wound often becomes infected, and the remedy is then worse than the original disease. Chinese authorities believed that when acupuncture was not suitable, moxa could be employed. One authority, Wang Tao of the T'ang dynasty discarded acupuncture in favor of moxa on the ground that the former was by then a lost art and was often accompanied by risks. Both practices were carried to Japan in the sixth century.

According to one belief early Portuguese navigators carried the ancient practices from Japan to the West. A number of nonmedical travelers and historians, including Bontius, Grossier, and Lord McCartney, also mentioned these methods of treatment. However, it is clear that acupuncture was actually introduced into European medicine when Ten Rhyne's dissertation was published in 1683 (2). (His name is given as Willem Ten Rhijne in Dutch.) Ten Rhyne was born in Deventer and ultimately entered the medical school at Leyden, where his doctoral thesis was on intestinal pain and gas. After graduation he joined the Dutch East India Company for service on the island of Java. His inquiring mind and facility in observation were quickly revealed when, during a stopover at Capetown, he collected botanical material (among the earliest from this region) and took notes for his essay on the Hottentots. He arrived at Jakarta and taught anatomy to the Dutch physicians there for six months. He sailed for Nagasaki, Japan, in June 1674. At that time the Dutch were the only Europeans allowed into the country. Japan had been closed to the rest of the world in 1641, but the ruler decided that some contact with the West would be beneficial. Spain and Portugal, notorious for their unscrupulous imperialism, were excluded. The English had tried to establish trade and failed. That left only the Dutch, who were allowed from 1641 on to maintain a closely guarded post on Dejima, near Nagasaki; the post included one doctor, who, from 1674 on, was Ten Rhyne. The Dutch were supposed to remain ignorant of Japanese language and life, but they learned a great deal from their own Japanese interpreters and from Japanese physicians who entered the compound surreptitiously to learn Western medicine. In addition, once a year, the Dutch made a slow 600-mile trip to Tokyo to tell the Emperor about the outside world, and this trip, together with their stay in Tokyo, afforded additional opportunities to acquire information. Sometime in 1674 and later, Ten Rhyne evidently discussed Dutch medicine with a Japanese physician, and an English version was published in Japan in 1680. Ten Rhyne also wrote important works on botany and on medical subjects during and after his residence on the island of Java, where he had returned for a time in 1674, as Carruba and Bowers have discussed (3).

Another Dutchman, Engelbertus Kaempfer, physician to the Dutch Embassy to the Court of the Emperor of Japan in 1712 wrote on the subject of acupuncture in an early work (4). He also brought back from Japan a manuscript "written in High-Dutch" of the history of Japan (5). It was published in two handsome volumes in 1727 with the imprimatur of Hans

Sloane, President of the Royal Society of London. The appendix to Volume II contains a section entitled *Of the Cure of Cholick by Acupunctura, or Needle-pricking as it is used by the Japanese.* This section includes diagrams showing the locations for insertion of the needles. A French edition, in three volumes but without most of the illustrations, was published in 1732.

Interest in acupuncture flagged for a time but soon revived strongly. Dujardin's history of surgery (6) brought it to notice once more, and after the treatises of Berlioz (7), Churchill (8), and Cloquet (9) were published, there was a resurgence of interest in the subject. This phase of its history is today largely ignored.

One of Cloquet's pupils, Dr. S. Morand, wrote a treatise (10) that when translated became the introduction of acupuncture into America. Although acupuncture was mentioned as early as 1820 in book reviews and other notices published in this country as Cassedy (11) noted, the matter was not presented in detail until Franklin Bache published the English translation of Morand's work in Philadelphia in 1825 (10). The circumstances that led to this publication were reported by Bache (10):

> The original of the present Memoir was put into my hands by my friend, Dr. Samuel Brown, late Professor of the Practice of Physic in Transylvania University, with a request that I would prepare a translation of it for the American medical public. I readily acceded to his wishes, believing, with him, that a short treatise on Acupuncturation, from the growing importance of the remedy, and the great attention bestowed upon it in France, could not fail to be an acceptable present to American physicians.
>
> The present Memoir, after an historical introduction, proceeds to give an account of the manner of using the needle, and concludes with a number of cases, illustrative of its effects. Without going too much into detail, it imparts every requisite information to enable any practitioner to employ the remedy.

The following year Bache described his own experience in a paper published in the *North American Medical and Surgical Journal* (12). Subsequently, other American physicians published case reports testifying to the good effects of acupuncture (despite which the *Boston Medical and Surgical Journal* stated in 1829 that the measure had "never crossed the Atlantic to this

new world"). Another French work, also translated and published in Philadelphia, also encouraged the use of acupuncture in
this country. This was Tavernier's *Elements of Operative Surgery*
(13). The Surgeon General's Index lists twenty-three books on
acupuncture published between 1823 and 1839 and also lists
dozens of papers on the subject. One early nineteenth-century
reference to acupuncture is found in the very first issue of
Lancet, Great Britain's famous medical journal. This issue, dated
October 5, 1823, contains a paper titled "Case of Anasarca
Successfully Treated by Acupuncturation."

Nevertheless the procedure was not universally praised. An
early nineteenth century print in the collection of the Boston
Medical Library shows a large pincushion on the floor, some
pins having been removed from it and inserted in several sick
people, one of whom has thrown his crutches away and is
dancing wildly. On the rear wall of the room is a picture of the
patron saint of acupuncturists, St. Sebastian on the day of his
martyrdom, full of arrows.

A number of influential texts published just after the middle
of the nineteenth century referred to acupuncture as a useful
form of treatment for certain diseases. The *Traité de Thérapeutique* by Trousseau and Pidoux (14) contains a thorough
discussion of the subject, including its history. In America, an
authoritative text was written by George B. Wood, professor of
Medicine at the University of Pennsylvania, president of the
Philadelphia College of Physicians, and former president of the
American Medical Association. This *Treatise on Therapeutics and
Pharmacology, or Materia Medica* (15) contains what is clearly
the best statement on the subject. Wood wrote:

> Acupuncture consists in the introduction of sharply pointed and very
> smooth needles, through the skin, into the tissues beneath. It is stated, as
> the result of numerous experiments, that all kinds of structure, muscles,
> blood-vessels, nerves, parenchymatous tissue, membranes, even the brain,
> may be thus penetrated without serious injury, if the needle be not allowed
> to remain too long. The sharp point seems to insinuate itself in such a
> mode as scarcely to wound, but merely to separate the ultimate
> components of the tissues. Steel needles are perhaps on the whole
> preferable, as being the sharpest, and susceptible of a very high polish; but
> silver, platinum, and gold have been recommended; and the two last have
> the advantage that they undergo no chemical change.

The introduction of the needle is, in some instances, apparently painless, in others very painful; but, in most, it produces a moderate uneasiness, which the patient finds easily supportable. Almost always a little redness and heat are perceptible about the place of the insertion. If allowed to continue, the needles often produce considerable inflammation in their course.

When the space to be operated on is limited, only a single needle is introduced; when it is extensive, several.

In the introduction of the needle, the skin should be rendered tense, the point gradually insinuated, and the instrument rotated between the fingers.

The length of time, during which the needles should be allowed to remain, varies with the effect. In simple neuralgia, they may afford relief in five or six minutes; in more fixed affections, often not before half an hour or an hour; and sometimes days elapse before the end is accomplished: but the rule is to allow them to remain until the pain is relieved. There is, however, some risk of injurious results from inflammation, if they are suffered to continue too long.

The complaints in which they have been most effectual are those of a neuralgic, rheumatic, and spasmodic character. The needle is introduced into the painful tissue.

How does acupuncture operate? I have no doubt whatever that in many instances, it acts through the mind, as the cold steel of the dentist will cure the toothache before the tooth has been pulled, or as the metallic tractors, and the homeopathic globules cure neuralgia and rheumatism. The relief is not the less positive because thus obtained. Perhaps there is still a revulsive action. The excitation of the cerebral nervous centres, diminishes irritation elsewhere; and, if the impression has been sufficiently strong, the relief may have a considerable degree of permanence.

But I am quite disposed to believe that there is also a more limited revulsion; the irritation which produces the pain of the disease, being diverted from its original seat towards the course of the instrument.

In another place Wood described the use of electricity with the needles, a practice still used in China today by radicals determined to bring Chinese technology up to date.

Wood's dedication is interesting. It reads:

To my dear friend, Franklin Bache, M.D., professor of chemistry in the Jefferson Medical College of Philadelphia; late president of the American Philosophical Society; my partner in much labour; my companion in many social hours; whom in the course of an intimate acquaintance of more than thirty years, I have never known to do an unjust act, or cherish an unjust thought; the accurate man of science; the skillful teacher; the upright and honorable man; and, in all points, the gentleman, I inscribe this work, in testimony of my profound esteem and sincere affection.

It is evident that Bache's opinions influence Wood greatly.

Another influential discussion of acupuncture in English is found in Sidney Ringer's *Handbook of Therapeutics*. This book was used by almost all English-speaking physicians, and went through many editions. The fourth edition (published in 1875) has a footnote recommending the insertion of needles into the muscles in the treatment of lumbago. This is repeated in the seventh edition (1879), but in addition, this edition, has a whole section headed "On Acupuncture" (16). It states that "acupuncture is a very successful mode of treating lumbago. It will rarely fail to afford relief, and in the majority of cases it will cure at once, though the lumbago has lasted a week, or even three weeks. . . . I have treated a large number of such cases by acupuncture and find it gives almost instantaneous relief." So weighty was the authority of Ringer's name that several decades later William Osler recommended the treatment in his textbook of medicine (17), probably the most widely used in the world at that time.

A curious misapplication of the term "acupuncture" occurs in Brown's 1869 treatise (18). Dr. Brown invented a device for introducing medications through the skin by means of a cluster of short needles, down which medications (which he sold separately) ran from a reservoir on top of the needles. Evidently the word acupuncture was sufficiently popular to induce him to appropriate the term for his own process. It was popular among physicians for a time.

It is evident that acupuncture was recommended by some of the outstanding medical authorities of the nineteenth century. It seems to have been used widely on the Continent, but much less in America. In any case, by the end of the nineteenth century, enthusiasm for the procedure had almost totally disappeared in this country. Infection was a common complication of its use. Perhaps the benefit did not occur often enough, or if it did occur, it did not last. Moreover, the pharmaceutical industry was beginning to produce effective analgesics to be taken by mouth. Thus, after two centuries of recognition in Europe, acupuncture died out almost a hundred years ago.

REFERENCES

1. Wong, K. C., and Wu, L-T. *History of Chinese medicine.* Tientsin, China: Tientsin Press, 1932.
2. Ten Rhyne, W. *Dissertatio de arthritide: Mantissa schematica: de acupunctura: et orationes tres, I De chymiae ac botaniae antiquitate & dignitate, II De physiognomia, III De monstris.* London: K. Chiswell (for the Royal Society), 1683.
3. Carruba, R. W., and Bowers, J. Z. The Western world's first detailed treatise on acupuncture: Willem Ten Rhyne's *De Acupunctura Journal of the History of Medicine and Allied Sciences* 29:371-398, 1974.
4. Kaempfer, E. *Histoire naturelle, civile, et ecclésiastique de l'Empire du Japon.* 3 volumes. Amsterdam: Herman Uttwerf, 1732.
5. Kaempfer, E. *The history of Japan.* J. G. Scheuchzer, trans. London: For the translator, 1727.
6. Dujardin, *Histoire de la chirurgie, depuis son origine jusqu'à nos jours.* Vol. 1. Paris: Royal Press, 1774, pp. 95 ff.
7. Berlioz, V. J. *Mémoire sur les maladies chroniques, les evacuations sanguines, et l'acupuncture.* Paris: Croulle Bois, 1816.
8. Churchill, J. M. A. *Treatise in acupuncturation: being a description of a surgical operation originally peculiar to the Japanese and Chinese, and by them denominated Zin-King, now introduced into European practice, with directions for its performance, and cases illustrating its success.* London: Simpkin and Marshall, 1823.
9. Cloquet, J. *Traité de l'acupuncture.* D. de Vannes, ed. Paris: Bechet Jeune, 1826.
10. Morand, S. *Memoir on acupuncturation, embracing a series of cases drawn up under the inspection of M. Julius Cloque; Paris, 1825.* F. Bache, trans. Philadelphia: R. Desilver, 1825.
11. Cassedy, J. H. Early uses of acupuncture in the United States, with an addendum (1826) by Franklin Bache, M.D. *Bulletin of the New York Academy of Medicine* 50:892-906, 1974.
12. Bache, F. Cases illustrative of the medical effects of acupuncturation. *North American Medical Surgical Journal* 1:311, 1826.
13. Tavernier, A. *Elements of operative surgery.* S. D. Gross, trans. and ed. Philadelphia: Collins and Hannay, Collins, Roorbach, 1829, pp. 55-57.
14. Trousseau, A., and Pidoux, H. *Traité de thérapeutique et de matière médicale.* 9th ed. Paris: P. Asselin, 1877.
15. Wood, G. B. *A treatise on therapeutics and pharmacology or materia medica.* Philadelphia: Lippincott, 1856.
16. Ringer, S. A. *A handbook on therapeutics.* 7th ed. New York: W. Wood, 1879, 87-90.
17. Osker, W., and McRae, T. *Modern medicine.* Philadelphia: Lea and Febiger, 1907.
18. Brown, A. R. *Treatise on acupuncturation, inoculation, diversion, and direct medical administration.* Albion, Mich.: A. R. Brown, 1869.

Chapter 9

THE CALCIFIED
PINEAL GLAND
nature mimics art—almost

The cure for lunacy.

The cure for folly (both paintings by Hierony-mous Bosch).

A number of paintings and prints made chiefly during the sixteenth through eighteenth centuries in the Low Countries and adjacent lands show medical quacks pretending to remove stones from within the heads of mentally abnormal persons. The earliest of these appears to be Bosch's *The Cure of Folly*, painted between 1475 and 1480 and now in the Prado Museum, in Madrid. This painting is perhaps ambiguous because no stone is visible. However, a later painting by Bosch, this one in the Rijks museum in Amsterdam, shows a bystander staring at the extracted stone, which he holds in his hand. A succession of painting and engravings by later artists who worked in or near the Low Countries followed these two (1). These subsequent works were by Jan Steen (three paintings), Frans Hals the Younger, David Teniers, Adriaen Brouwer, Andries Both, Abraham Diepraem, Frans van Mieris, Peter Bruegel the Elder, Theodore de Bry, Nicolaes Weydmans, Jan van den Bruggen, Cornelis de Wael, Jan van Hemmessen, Crispin de Passe, Ellias Haid, Pieter Balden, and a number of others who cannot today be named. The persons being so treated in all the earliest works were men, and it was not until H. Weydmans created his print in the seventeenth century that women gained the right of equal representation. However, even in this instance male chauvinism cannot be excluded, for the inscription beneath the Weydmans print has been translated as "Come, come with great rejoicing; here the stones can be cut out of your wife."

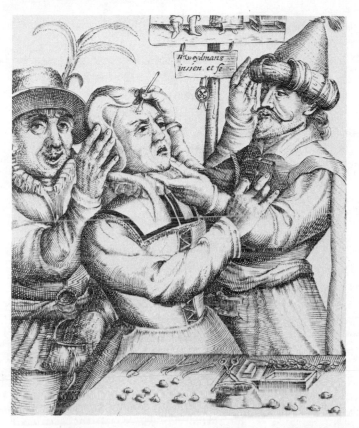

Operation for stone in the head, an engraving by H. Weydmans.

The origin of the superstition seems fairly clear. Although
trephining for mental disease had been practiced from pre-
historic times (and well into the twentieth century), it is
unlikely that this alone led to the belief about the stones. This
particular superstition was apparently owing to a double meaning of the Dutch word *kieje*. In Bosch's painting the caption
reads "Meister snijt die kicjc ras," which can be translated in
two ways, either "Master, cut the stone out" or "Master, cut the
problem out." Thus was the slang phrase "rocks in the head"
conceived, if perhaps not yet born.

At the same time another superstition more specifically
medical was also developing. It involved a purported relation
between the formation of stones in the pineal gland and the

development of insanity. This notion was probably introduced or, at any rate, initially supported by Théophile Bonet of Geneva. In order to understand how this medical superstition arose, it is necessary to understand why Bonet was interested in a possible relation between pineal disease and insanity.

This assumed relation had its roots in some ancient beliefs about the mind or soul. In the fifth century B.C. Anaxagoras stated that the soul of man resided in the ventricles of the brain, a belief that Herophilus echoed two centuries later. It is probable that Herophilus first described the pineal gland and that either he or one of his followers enunciated the idea that it might have a role in thinking, because he believed that it controlled the flow of *pneuma*. (The idea that it might control the flow of something persisted for many centuries; Riolan (2) mentioned it in his textbook of anatomy published in 1648, and Wharton (3) in his text published in 1665. Magendie (4) in the early nineteenth century and von Cyon (5) in the early twentieth century believed that it regulated the flow of the spinal fluid.) However, Galen (6), the greatest physician of the Roman era, derogated the idea that the pineal gland regulated the flow of pneuma in the brain:

> Returning to the parts that come after the middle ventricle, we will consider the body situated at the entrance to the canal, the body that connects this ventricle to the cerebellum which is called *conarium* (the pineal gland) by those who concern themselves with dissections, and we shall seek to ascertain for what purpose this body has been created. Judging by its substance, it is a gland. In shape, it is very like a pine cone, whence comes its name.
>
> Some believe that its use is the same as that of the pylorus. They claim that the *conarium*, situated at the entrance to the canal that transmits the *pneuma* from the middle ventricle into the ventricle of the cerebellum, is the watcher and is a sort of guardian that decides how much *pneuma* should be transmitted. . . .
>
> But to believe that the *conarium* regulates the passage of the spirit is to misconstrue the function of the vermiform apophysis (the inferior vermis of the cerebellum) and to attribute to a gland more than its true importance. In effect, if it constituted a part of the encephalon itself, as the pylorus constitutes a part of the stomach, its favorable position would enable it to open and close the conduit in obedience to the contractions and dilations of this encephalon. Since, on the contrary, the gland does not in any way constitute a part of the encephalon, and since it is attached not

to the inside of the ventricle but exteriorly, how could it have so powerful an action on the conduit when it does not move itself?

When one thinks, in fact, that there should necessarily exist near the canal of the cerebrum a proper part to watch and regulate the entrance of the *pneuma*, that part, which one cannot discern, is not the *conarium* but that worm-like apophysis that extends along the whole conduit. The clever anatomists, giving it a name derived from its shape, call it the vermicular apophysis.

Galen's description of the anatomical relations of the pineal gland used a genital symbolism which apparently was widely accepted by ancient anatomists, as will be discussed later.

The tenth-century Galenist Costa ben Luca (or Kosta ben Luka, or Constabulus, or Constabulinus) of Baalbek repeated Galen's ideas (7). Ben Luca wrote:

The brain is divided into divisions, of which one is in front, and is the larger, and the other is in the rear. In the front division there are two ventricles, having an opening to a common space which is the middle of the brain.

In the passage and road, that is, in the entrance through which the *pneuma* passes, there is a space, and a little particle of the body of the brain, like a worm, which is lifted and let down in the path. When the particle is lifted up, the hole is opened. . . . When therefore the hole is open, the *pneuma* passes from the front of the brain to the rear, and this does not happen except when it is necessary to remember something which was given over to forgetfulness, at the time when thought is being taken about past things.

Ben Luca added that men who wish to recall something shake their heads in order to loosen the memory valve. (These observations proved conclusively that the valve existed. Unfortunately his data are not available now and hence the p values cannot be calculated.)

Ben Luca's works were translated into Latin by Johann Avendeath (Ibn Dawed, the Jewish scholar of Toledo), and his ideas were enthusiastically adopted by such influential teachers as William of Conches.

In 1316 Mondino dei Lucci (Mundinus) finished his compendium of anatomy (8). Although he probably had dissected several human bodies, he based most of his writing on Greek and Arabic sources; his description of the brain and its functions

were Galenic. Mondino mentioned the pineal gland but maintained that the flow of thought was regulated by a "red worm,"
the choroid plesus. The commentary on Mondino written by
Giacomo Berengario da Carpi also mentioned the pineal gland
and the *thought worm* (9). The idea of a thought worm was still
accepted at least as late as 1575; it was represented in an
illustration in Lodovico Dolce's treatise on how to conserve the
memory. (This illustration resembles one that Singer reproduced
from G. Reisch's *Margarita philosophiae*, printed in Freiburg in
1503.)

Descartes reestablished a connection between the pineal
gland and mental function when he declared the gland to be the
seat of the soul. What was probably the first expression of this
idea appeared in a letter sent to Father Mersenne for transmission to the physician Meissonnier of Lyons (10). Descartes
named the pineal gland the seat of the soul because he believed
that the soul had to reside in an unpaired structure in the brain.
(If it did not, we would see, hear, smell, taste, and feel
everything double, he stated.) The pituitary gland was ruled out
because it was completely involved in the superstitious belief
that the brain formed mucus, which had to be expelled by the

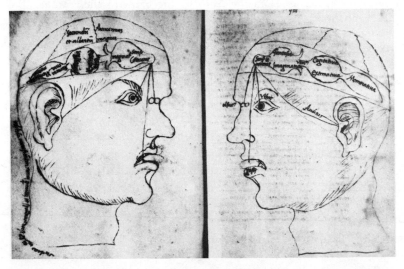

*Drawing from a sixteenth-century manuscript, showing the mental faculties
situated in various parts of the brain; memory is in the rearmost ventricle.*

pituitary gland through the nose to prevent migration of the mucus to other parts of the body where it would cause the dreaded "catarrh."

Descartes's idea was published in detail in 1662, twelve years after his death. His own account, written in *Les Passions de l'Ame* in 1649, has been translated as follows (11):

Article 31

That there is a small gland in the brain in which the soul exercises its function more specifically than in its other parts.

We have also to bear in mind that although the soul is joined to the whole body, there is yet in the body a certain part in which it exercises its functions more specifically than in all the others. It is a matter of common belief that this part is the brain, or possibly the heart—the brain because of its relation to the senses, the heart because it is there that we feel the passions. But on carefully examining the matter, I seem to find evidence that the part of the body in which the soul exercises its functions immediately is in no wise the heart, nor the brain as a whole, but solely the innermost part of the brain, viz. a certain very small gland, situated in a midway position, and suspended over the passage by which the animal spirits of the anterior cavities communicate with those of the posterior cavities, in such fashion that its slightest movements can greatly alter the course of those spirits: and reciprocally that any change, however slight, taking place in the course of the spirits can greatly change the movements of this gland.

Article 32

How we know this to be the chief seat of the soul.

The reason which persuades me that the soul cannot have anywhere in the body any other location for the immediate exercise of its functions is that I observe all the other parts of the brain to be double, just as we have two eyes, two hands, two ears, and indeed all the organs of our external senses double; and that since of any one thing at any one time we have only one single and simple thought, there must be some place where the two images come from one single object by way of the double organs of the other senses, can unite before reaching the soul, and so prevent their representing it to two objects in place of one. We can easily think of these images or other impressions as being united in this gland by mediation of the spirits which fill the cavities of the brain. There is no other place in the brain save only this gland, where they can be thus united.

Article 42

How we find in the memory the things we wish to remember.

Thus when the soul wills to recall something, this volition, by causing the gland to bend successively now to one side and now to another, impels the spirits towards this and that region of the brain, until they come upon the part where the traces left by the object we will to recall are found. These traces consist in the manner in which the spirits, owing to the paths they have taken on the presence of that object, have so modified the pores of the brain that these have thereby acquired a greater facility than the others of being opened in that same fashion when the spirits again come towards them. The spirits on meeting these pores therefore enter into them more easily than into the others, and thereby excite that special movement in the gland which represents that same object to the soul, and so enable it to know what it has willed to remember.

Descartes believed that the pineal gland extracted the animal spirits from the arteries, transmitted them to the cerebral ventricles, and distributed them throughout the body by the way of the nerves (then believed to be tubes). The pineal gland not only secreted the animals spirits, he thought, but also regulated their distribution by moving to one side or the other. An anonymous treatise (12) appeared in 1685 that combined these ideas with the then developing knowledge of the blood's circulation; its author suggested a scheme of circulation of animal spirits from the ventricles of the brain, through the nerves, and then back to the pineal gland by way of the tissue lymphatics, the veins, the heart, and the carotid arteries.

It must be remembered that Descartes had gone to live with his grandfather after the death of his mother when he was only one year old. His grandfather was a highly respected physician, and as Descartes was growing up, he probably had access to medical books. In addition, as an adult, he numbered among his closest friends Dr. Isaac Beeckman. Among the important medical books of that period were Du Laurens' *Historia Anatomica Humani Corporis* (13) published in Latin in 1600 and translated into French in 1621, and Daniel Sennert's writings of about the same time (14). (Sennert, "that able clinician," was the first to describe scarlet fever.) Although Sennert mentioned the occurrence of calcification in the brain, he did not associate this finding with any disease, and did not mention the pineal gland at all. Du Laurens echoed Galen's words:

In this conduit several particles present themselves, and first a small gland of pointed shape rather similar to a pine cone, which has been named by the Greeks *conoide* and *conarion*: It is believed to serve, as do the other glands, to fasten the veins and arteries that are distributed in the cerebrum, to the end that the animal spirit has a free and open road to go from the third ventricle to the fourth. Behind the *Conarion*, contiguous to one part or another, are certain small round and hard bodies which are called from their form in Greek *gloutia*, in Latin *nates*, that is to say, the buttocks; below which appear the testicles named by the Greeks *orcheis* and *didumoi*, and by the Latins *testes*. Their function is to form the canal that goes from the third to the fourth, and to give safe-conduit (as one says) to the animal spirit. Finally there presents itself the fourth ventricle, common to the cerebellum and the spinal marrow; which is the smallest and the most solid of all. This ventricle is at first larger, it narrows gently until it terminates, like a quill pen, which Herophilus calls *calamus*. As regards the *vermiform epiphysis*, it is not part of the cerebrum but of the cerebellum, and holds open the road from the third ventricle to the fourth.

Du Laurens negated the idea that the choroid plexus was a thought valve when he added: "They are wrong to opine that it is the unbound meningus that is gathered and contracted and that it is necessary that it extends itself in the dilatation, and that it gathers together and folds in the contraction of the brain." The illustrations used by du Laurens were after those of Vesalius, and were in striking contrast to the childish diagrams later used by Descartes. Although du Laurens stated, "I say then that the principal seat of the soul is in the brain," he did not localize it in any part.

Crooke's treatise (15), published in 1616, was in large part modeled after that of du Laurens. After noting that the gland's shape resembled that "of a Pine-apple" and that it was accordingly named *Glandula Pinealis*, Crooke called it "the Pine-glandule" and so designated it in the accompanying ana-tomical drawing. Of course, neither du Laurens nor Crooke discussed Descartes's notions about the function of the gland.

Descartes's concept was attacked from various directions. Although Vieussens (16) and some others accepted the idea that the pineal gland secreted animal spirits, Ridley (17) said that the pineal gland was "a very unfit part to be made a Receptacle for Animal Spirits, as Vieussenius makes it, and much more a place of residence for the soul according to Des Chartes." Kenelm Digby (18) rejected the idea that the soul resided in the gland. He wrote, "This part [septum lucidum] seems to me (after weighing all circumstances and considering all the conveniences and fitnesses) to be that, and only that, in which the fansie or common sense resides; though Monsir des Cartes has rather chosen a kernel to place it in." (Digby's notion was in part based on the erroneous belief that there was a ventricle between the two layers of the septum lucidum.) Others who still preferred to believe that the soul resided in the ventricles were More (19) and Soemmering (20). Lancisi (21), on the other hand, held that the corpus callosum was the seat of the soul because, it seemed to him, there was a close relation between diseases of that structure and death. Lancisi's notion was not widely accepted; Charles Bonnet (22) mentioned it but without enthusiasm, and Haller (23) rejected it.

Descartes's ideas about the function of the pineal gland also were decried by seventeenth- and eighteenth-century anatomists such as Wharton (3), Bartholin (24), and Gibson (25). Gibson said that this was "too noble a use for it." Le Camus (26) also derogated Descartes's ideas, saying that the whole brain undoubtedly secreted the animal spirits from the blood. The attitude of the anatomists was summarized by Gibson (25) in 1682. He wrote:

The first is *Glandula pinealis*, or Penis, because it representeth the Pine-nut, or a Man's Yard. It is seated in the beginning of the Pipe, by which the third and fourth Ventricles are united. Its basis is downwards, and its apex or end looks upward. It is of a substance harder than the Brain, of a pale colour and covered with a thin Membrane. This Gland *des Cartes* thinks to be the primary seat of the Soul, and that all animal operations draw their origins from it. But Bartholin has sufficiently confuted that opinion; for it seems to be but of the same use as other Glands, and particularly the Glandula pituitaria placed near it, viz. to separate the *Lympha* from the Arterial blood; which *Lympha* is absorbed by the Veins (or it may be by *Vasa lymphatica*) as shown from Dr. Lower. Near to this on both sides of this third Ventricle four round bodies appear. The two upper are lesser, and are called *Testes*: the two greater are lower, and are called *Nates*. The clink betwixt the *Nates* is called *Anus*.

Not only had the leading anatomists of the seventeenth century rejected the idea that the pineal gland was the seat of the soul, but there was in addition considerable opposition to the idea that the soul had any particular seat within the brain. Thus the anatomist Vesalius, the physiologist Haller, and the philosopher de la Mettrie all agreed with Du Laurens in this respect. De la Mettrie (27) used language which by then had become commonplace, when he wrote in 1745: "Those who place the seat of the Soul in the *nates* or the *testes*, are they more wrong than those who wish to establish it in the *centrum ovale*, or even in the pineal gland?"

Haller (29) in 1759 actually used Galen's language to describe the region of the pineal gland:

It is marked behind by four oval eminences, which are outwardly smaller, called the nates and testes, and which consist externally of some medulla, and internally of cortical substance. The superior ones in man are the largest and are called the nates. Upon these is seated a cortical gland, ovally conical, supplied with many vessels, into which the choroid plexus disappears: This is [the] celebrated pineal gland so frequently diseased, which is joined to the brain by small footstalks.

A few pages later, Haller added, "The seat of the mind must be where the nerves first begin."

Skepticism about the seat of the soul being in the pineal gland seemed to increase. The satirical memoirs (28) of Martin Scriblerus, head of the mythical Scriblerus Club, state:

Calves and Philosophers, Tygers and Statesmen, Foxes and Sharpers, Peacocks and Fops, Cock-Sparrows and Coquets, Monkeys and Players, Courtiers and Spaniels, Moles and Misers, exactly resemble one another in the conformation of the *Pineal Gland.* He did not doubt likewise to find the same resemblances in Highwaymen and Conquerors.

The famous physician Radcliffe, advised Richard Mead on "How to Get a Practice" (29):

A physician should never affect ignorance of the cause of a complaint; he should place it in the pancreas, or pineal gland, if he has no other local habitations available at the moment.

Even when an intelligent layman adopted the Cartesian notion, it was lightly and almost mockingly. An anonymous collection of anecdotes (30) "medical, chemical and chirurgical," published in 1816, contains the following passage:

Glandula Pinealis

In the letters of Brossette to Racine, my be found the following passage: After a peaceable and happy union with Margueret Chavigny during ten years, Brossette had the misfortune to lose her. He thought he could not better testify how dear the deceased was to him, than by carrying on his person a part of her. To this end, he caused the pineal gland to be drawn from her brain, had it enclosed in the collet of a golden ring, and carried it on his finger the rest of his life. He directed by his will that this ring should be buried with him. It may be remarked, that Brossette is, perhaps, the only husband who has preserved the relics of his wife. No Orpheus, now-a-days, goes to hell to search for his Eurydice.

Consideration of these events makes it difficult to understand how, in the face of all the medical and other negation, a medical version of the brain-stone superstition could have become firmly established, which it did. It is probable that the explanation of what happened lies in the personalities of some leaders in the world of scholars. One of these, Claude Clerselier, the book publisher of Geneva, was important in this regard. He was a friend and admirer of René Descartes. After the death of Father Mersenne, with whom Descartes had been corresponding for years, Clerselier replaced the learned priest as Descartes's chief correspondent, the man who served as the main sounding board for Descartes's ideas. Clerselier was a great admirer of Descartes, and after his death edited and published many writings not previously brought out. Some of these were the works that helped to spread Descartes's reputation as a philosopher and mathematician. Clerselier had a considerable amount of evangelism in him. For example, his son-in-law, Jacques Rohault, a wealthy young man of Amiens, was a student of philosophy and mathematics, and apparently influenced by his wife's father, he became converted to Cartesian ideas, and expounded them in his *Traité de Physique* in 1671 (31). This work was highly successful and was perhaps the means of advancing Cartesian ideas over the powerful resistance of those who held to earlier systems. It is said that the attacks of his enemies led to Rohault's early death, before which he was refused extreme unction until he made a new profession of Catholic faith. (After his death, Clerselier edited and published others of his works, just as he had done for Descartes.) Rohault's *Traité* was published in French in about a dozen editions. It was also translated into English. In order to make it available to scholars everywhere, the decision was made to have it translated into Latin. This was done by Théophile Bonet, the Genevan physician. Bonet was not only a member of Clerselier's circle of enthusiastic Cartesians, he was also one of the most prolific and widely read medical teachers of his era. Whereas other great clinical teachers of the era made their reputations by bedside teaching and by training disciples, some of whom became great in turn, Bonet gained his fame from his writings.

Bonet was also the compiler of a massive amount of clinicopathologic correlative data gathered from the literature. His book *Sepulchretum* (32) was praised by Morgagni, who also expressed his admiration for the author and his indebtedness to him. It is easy to imagine the feelings of this enthusiastic follower of Descartes when during his extensive reading in the medical literature, Bonet encountered a case of insanity apparently associated with unusual hardness of the pineal gland. Nature seemed to have provided proof to support Descartes's ideas about the seat of the soul. Bonet had not himself actually seen a case of the type under discussion, and his reference is to one published by Zwinger. Zwinger stated that a patient of his who had been psychotic for many years had been found after death to have had an unusually hard pineal gland.

Although earlier authors such as Regnier de Graaf of Schoonhaven and Charles Drelincourt of Leyden had reported around 1670 that the pineal gland often became calcified, they did not connect this fact with any clinical syndrome. However, Bonet's reputation gave his ideas great force and the consequences of Bonet's publication are evident. In 1686 Sir Edmund King of London (physician to George I) wrote of his observations on a petrified *glandula pinealis* found in the dissection of a brain, in *Nouvelles de la République des Lettres* for April 1687 (the letter was dated November 6, 1686). It carried the news throughout the civilized world. Dr. King said that although he has dissected one hundred brains, he had never before seen or heard of anything like this one. His patient had been suffering from "fatuitas" during life. (Fatuitas later came to be called dementia praecox.) King's account was also published in the *Philosophical Transactions of the Royal Society* (33). In 1753, Günz, physician to the King of Poland and councilor to the Elector of Saxony, published a treatise describing the pineal glands of five insane persons as having been turned to little stones (34). The great Morgagni reported that calcific masses which resemble congeries of small stones were to be found in the pineal glands of some insane persons. He also referred to the earlier report of Bonet and mentioned an additional instance of pineal calcification associated with psychosis described by Berlingerius Gipseus. In the latter instance, the gland was entirely turned to stone. Morgagni (35) stated that calcification "had been found with madness and without it also, yet I would not have you forget there is not any one disorder wherewith it is so frequently to be join'd as with madness." Arnold's *Observations on Insanity* (36) discussed Morgagni's findings in detail. Arnold's book contains (on page 75) a table of the bodily causes of mental disease, among which is "stony hardness of the pineal gland." However, Soemmering (37) and Baillie (38) both stated again that calcification of the pineal gland was a normal finding. Despite this, Crichton (39) in 1798 and Haslam (40) as late as 1809 wrote that some patients with mental disease had abnormally calcified pineal glands. Bucknill and Tuke (41) in 1858 noted Morgagni's remarks but made no comment on them.

But the tide had begun to turn. The great J. F. Meckel (42) won a prize for a treatise on the cause of insanity, in which he stated that the psychotic brain had a higher than normal specific gravity. Although he recorded finding granules of calcific material in the pineal glands of some of the patients, many did not have them. In fact, in his *Manual of Anatomy* (43), he stated clearly that calcifications in the pineal gland were a normal finding. A succession of authors in the first half of the nineteenth century published reports on large numbers of post-mortem examinations and also stated that pineal calcification was common in normal persons and could not have anything to do with mental disease. The bubble burst quickly. All that remains today of the superstition concerning rocks in the head is the slang expression.

REFERENCES

1. Miège, H. L'opération des pierres de tête. *Aesculape* 22:50, 1932.
2. Riolan, J. *Encheiridium anatomicum et pathologicum.* Leyden: A. Wyngaerden, 1649, pp. 248 ff.
3. Wharton, T. *Adenographia, sive glandularum totius corporis descriptio.* London: J. G., 1656, p. 149.
4. Magendie, F. *Recherches physiologiques, et cliniques sur le fluide céphalorachidien ou cérébrospinal.* Paris: Méquignon-Marvis Fils, 1842.
5. Von Cyon, E. Zur Physiologie der Zirbeldruse. *Archiv ges. Physiol.,* 98.927, 1908.
6. Galen, C. *Oeuvres anatomiques, physiologiques, et médicales.* Vol. 1. C. Daremberg, trans. Paris: J. B. Ballière, 1854, p. 564.
7. Ben Luca, C., in Klubertanz, G. P. *The discursive power, sources and doctrine of the Vis Cogitative according to St. Thomas Aquinas.* St. Louis, Mo.: Modern Schoolman, 1952.
8. Wickersheimer, E. *Anatomies de Mondino Dei Luzzi et de Guido de Vigevano.* Paris: E. Droz, 1926.
9. Berengario da Catpi, in Sarton, G. *Introduction to the history of Science.* Vol. 3. Washington, D.C.: Carnegie Institution, 1947, p. 844.
10. Descartes, R. *Oeuvres.* Vol. 8. Paris: F. G. Levrault, 1824–1826, p. 200.
11. Descartes, R. Les passiones de l'âme. In Reeves, J. W., *Body and mind in Western thought.* New York: Penquin Books, 1950, pp. 293–294.
12. Anonymous: Un réligieux de la congrégation de Saint Maur (Original publisher unknown; possibly Jamet). *Traité de la circulation des espirits animaux.* Paris: Louis Billaine, 1682.
13. Du Laurens, A. *Toutes les oeuvres.* Trans. from the 1605 Latin ed. by T. Gelée. Rouen: Du Petit Val, 1621.
14. Bonnet, C. *Epitome universam dan. Sennerti doctrinam. Colonia allobrogum.* Geneva: P. Gamenetus, 1655.
15. Crroke, H. *A description of the body of man.* Barbican: W. Iaggard, 1616, pp. 467 ff.
16. Vieussens, R. *Neurographia universalis.* Lyons: Certe, 1685.
17. Ridley H. *Anatomia cerelri*, Leyden: J. A. Langerok, 1725, pp. 84 ff.
18. Digby, K. *Of bodies, and of man's soul: To discover the immortality of reasonable souls.* London: John Williams, 1669.
19. More, H. The immortality of the soul. In *A collection of several philosophical writings of Dr. Henry More.* Cambridge, England: T. Worden, 1659.

20. Soemmering, S. T. *Ueber das Organ der Seele.* Koenigsberg: F. Nicolovius, 1796.
21. Lancisi, G. M. *Opera qua hactemis prodierunt amnia.* Geneva: De Tournes, 1718.
22. Bonnet, C. *Essai analytique sur les facultés de l'âme.* Copenhagen: C. and A. Philibert, 1760, pp. 552 ff.
23. Haller, A. *First lines of physiology.* Trans. from 3rd Latin ed. Troy: O. Penniman, 1803, pp. 167 ff.
24. Bartholin, C. *Institutiones anatomicae . . . .* Libri III. T. Bartholin, ed. Leiden: F. Hack, 1655, pp. 336 ff.
25. Gibson, T. *The anatomy of humane bodies epitomized.* London: A. & J. Churchill, 1682.
26. Le Camus, M. *Médecine de l'esprit.* Rev. ed. Paris: Ganeau, 1769, p. 132.
27. De la Mettrie, J. O. (Charp, pseud.) *Histoire naturelle de l'âme.* M. Haller, trans. La Haye: J. Neaulme, 1745.
28. Kerby-Miller, C. *The memoirs of Martinus Scriblerus.* New Haven: Yale University Press, 1950, p. 137.
29. In Anonymous. *Physic and physicians.* London: Longueau, Orme, 1839, Chapter 6.
30. An Adept. *Anecdotes medical, chemical, and chirurgical.* London: J. Callow, 1816
31. Rohault, J. *Traité de physique.* Paris: C. Savreux, 1671.
32. Bonet, T. *Sepulchretum sive anatomia practica.* Geneva: Cramer and Perachon, 1700.
33. King, E. A stone in the glandula pinealis. Philosophical transactions of the Royal Society of London 3:157, 1700. Paper presented at the session of December 1686.
34. Günz, J. G. *Pr indicit, ac simul lapillos glandulae pinealis in quinque mente alienatis inventos proponit.* Leipzig: Langenheim, 1753.
35. Morgagni, G. B. *The seats and causes of diseases.* B. Alexander, trans. London: A. Miller and T. Cadell, 1769, pp. 457 ff.
36. Arnold, T. *Observations on the nature, kinds, causes, and prevention of insanity, lunacy, or madness.* Vol. 2. Leicester: G. Ireland for G. Robinson and T. Cadell, 1786.
37. Soemmering, S. T. *Acervulo cerebri.* In F. L. Ludwig, *Scriptores neurologici minore.* Leipzig, 1793, p. 322.
38. Baillie, M. *The morbid anatomy of the most important parts of the human body.* London: D. Johnson and G. Niol, 1797, pp. 459 ff.
39. Crichton, A. *An inquiry into the nature and origin of mental derangement.* London: T. Cadell, Jr., and W. Davis, 1798.
40. Haslam, J. *Observations on madness and melancholy, including practical remarks on those diseases; together with cases and an account of the morbid appearance on dissection.* 2nd ed. London: J. Callow, 1809.

41. Bucknill, J. C., and Tuke, D. H. *A manual of psychological medicine.* Philadelphia: Lea and Blanchard, 1858, p. 397.
42. Meckel, J. F. Recherches anatomico-physiologiques sur les causes de la folie. *Memoirs de l'Académie Royale des Sciences de Berlin.* 16:Article 92, 1760.
43. Meckel, J. F. *Manual of general, descriptive and pathological anatomy.* New York: Sleight, 1831, p. 546.

Chapter 10

SWEDENBORG AND STAHL
opposite—and wrong—sides of the same coin

Emmanuel Swedenborg (left), a fiercely energetic inquiring mind, interested in many different aspects of nature, and Ernst Stahl (right), a rigid, over-whelmingly formal mind, believed by its owner and his disciples to be incapable of error. Stahl was overtly psychotic in the last years of his life.

Higher vertebrates, that is, birds and mammals, spend at least part of their lives in organized social groups. Chaos is avoided in these groups because the individuals in it arrange themselves in an order determined by strength or aggressiveness. This ensures an orderly, if not necessarily just, distribution of available food, water, shelter and, at certain times, sex.

Similar phenomena occur in human social groups, but there is another great factor that determines human behavior, namely, labeling. Courses taken at school or college, and academic certificates or degrees, are important determinants of the nature of one's label. Having acquired a label, men and women are expected to behave predictably in accordance with it, barring such accidental circumstances as a marriage, an inheritance, or an unbearable distaste for what one finds oneself doing. Occasionally, behavior deviates from the expected for another reason, namely, the idiosyncratic interpretation of the implications of one's label that a person may make. It sometimes happens that the way a person interprets what his career should be turns out to be markedly different from the traditional view of the career determined by his label. This was strikingly true of the two men discussed here.

There are surprising parallels and also important differences in the careers of two men, one a physician, Georg Ernst Stahl (1660-1734), and the other a physicist turned anatomist and finally spiritual teacher, Emanuel Swedenborg (1688-1772).

184

Both men had one thing in common, their belief about the human soul. This belief, originally stated by Plato, held that the soul was not merely a spiritual entity, presumedly immortal, but was the rational force that directed the creation of the body for its own purposes—that is, a seat of its own residence and an agency for carrying out its intentions.

The specifics of this general belief differed only in minor detail in the minds of the two men. But the ways in which the two men used this idea in formulating their views on the nature of human bodily functioning were totally opposite. It is ironic that the views of the physician Stahl were mystical, dogmatic, and unsupported by anything but stubborn insistence on the logical consequences of his reasoning, based on nonsensical assumptions. It is also ironic, but not surprising, that Stahl's views, after a certain amount of inspired but trivial semantic juggling, created the American psychosomatic medicine of the mid-twentieth century.

Our understanding of the state of mind as well as the frame of reference of the thinkers of the period requires some discussion of the philosophy that developed after the establishment of Christianity's dominance in Europe and the Middle East. The philosophers who created early Christian theology maintained that God had created a perfect world, while allowing, for some reason, for the introduction of imperfections from time to time by Satan. At any rate, all medieval theologians held, for instance, that depression was a sin because it resulted from failure to appreciate God's wonderful world (see Chapter 5). From the time of the post-Nicene neo Platonists on, this view was maintained, and man was regarded as a small, complex part (microcosm) of the total universe (macrocosm), which was the creation and expression of God's mind and will and always controlled man's state and actions. This view of the nature of man led to the rise of astrology in daily life and more particularly in medical diagnosis. Medieval physicians studied a patient's horoscope as avidly as today's physicians study the laboratory sheet in the patient's medical record. The result in both cases was that the patient was ignored. The Augustinian doctrine that the soul gives being and species to the body originated in earlier philosophies and strongly influenced medical thinking for more than a thousand years. (As did his predecessors in the Church, Augustine esteemed Plato more highly than he esteemed Aristotle through sympathy and not because he knew Aristotle incompletely.) Centuries later, when interest in studying nature developed, the function of observational science was held to be the gaining of knowledge about the nature of God and of man, but a positive knowledge of the existence of God, even to men like Francis Bacon, was a matter of faith. Attitudes were changing, however, in part because of the influence of the Protestant Reformation. Thus another seventeenth-century English philosopher, Thomas Hobbes, established the Sensist School, which maintained that only the evidence of the senses was acceptable. Thereafter, to many the existence of God became dependent on *argument from design*. According to this a•gument the existence of God was to be inferred from the wonderful perfection of structure and function of everything in the universe.* To those who already believed in God, scientific knowledge lent support (which strictly speaking was not necessary) to this belief and, more important, afforded information about the nature of God and his intentions toward the world and man. Emanuel Swedenborg, a devout Protestant, maintained this position.

Emanuel Swedenborg was a highly unusual man. Only the fact that his late writings took the direction of a mystical type of theology, a theology that many cannot understand, much less accept, has kept him from being recognized as one of the most remarkable minds in the history of man. Before he was fifty years old, he had established himself as one of Sweden's outstanding leaders in pure and applied physics, and in engineering during the reign of Charles XII and his successors. Among his many distinctions was membership in Sweden's Royal College of Mines. When he was in his late forties, his attention turned to anatomical studies, which he pursued from 1736 to 1740. After this, he produced the writings that led to

---

*The idea that the wonders of Nature not only reflected the glory of God but also proved his existence was widely but not universally accepted. One sixteenth-century thinker, Julius Caesar Vanini, rejected the idea, and was burned at the stake for his unorthodoxy. (See Hines, W. L., "Mersenne and Vanini." *Renaissance Quarterly* 39:52, 1976.)

his being considered solely a theologian and mystic, his earlier work pushed to the background. During a period of four years, Swedenborg published dozens of articles, some of monographic length, on what he learned from his close reading of all the anatomical works then current plus eighteen months of study at the Royal School of Surgery in Paris. In addition to reading anatomy, he performed dissections on animals. Swedenborg's anatomical writings revealed a remarkable ability to interpret anatomical findings in terms of the functions they subserved. For example, although Vieussens in 1706 and Thebesius in 1708 had shown that the Thebesian vessels in the heart carried off blood from the coronary vessels, Swedenborg maintained that they were tidal channels, able to conduct blood into the myocardium from the cardiac chambers, as Lancisi later discovered (1). In another direction, Swedenborg was the first to emphasize the primary role of the cerebral cortex in thought, sensation, and motion, when his contemporaries in medicine had other ideas, now thankfully forgotten, on these matters. Many of his physiologic conclusions from anatomical data preceded by decades or by a century or more the working out of these problems by physicians.

What led Swedenborg from his interest in physics, pure and applied, into this new area? The answer is evident in Swedenborg's writings. He firmly believed (as had Plato, and after him dozens of Christian thinkers since the early days of the Church) that the body existed only to serve as the soul's residence, that the soul had created it for this purpose. Since the nature of the soul had baffled all who had considered it, Swedenborg thought to learn about it by studying in meticulous detail the functioning of its residence, the body. His massive work, a collection of all his knowledge in this area, he called *Oeconomia Regni Animalis* (2), which has been translated as *Economy of the Animal Kingdom*. One wonders if a more appropriate translation, since Swedenborg was evidently influenced by Descartes's *De anima*, might be "Economy of the Soul's Kingdom," as Pratt (1) has pointed out.

This period of Swedenborg's career was meant to serve as the steppingstone to the next phase, his life as theologian and seer. His fame as theologian far overshadowed his position as physiological thinker. Moreover, Swedenborg was not a member of any medical faculty, not even a physician, and the writers of physician's texts scarcely referred to him. As his works were published, they were noted in the learned reviews of the time, and it is highly probable that they influenced, at least insofar as they indicated a method of study, the French thinkers of the mid-eighteenth century who also sought to penetrate the mystery of the soul, if any such thing existed. Hence, we must look to the works of laymen such as de Tracy, d'Holbach, and Bonnet, and the like, for Swedenborg's influence rather than in writings of great medical compilers such as Haller. In addition, of course, other lay followers created a new religion in accordance with his new theology.

Swedenborg's writings reveal him as a nonscientist who believed firmly in the existence of the soul, and who accumulated vast stores of scientific information to help him in his inquiries.

Georg Ernst Stahl was quite a different type. A native of Bavaria, he rose to the professorship of medicine at Halle, and became chief physician to Frederic William I. He was a man of great strength of character, who expounded nonsense with all the authority of an incorrect clock striking wrong hours. For example, his theory of combustion held that a burning substance gave up a hypothetical phlogiston, thus becoming dephlogisticated. He believed this despite the fact that it had already been shown that a burned substance, if not volatilized, gains weight. This led to the absurd notion that the hypothetical *phlogiston* had negative weight. The phlogiston theory held back the progress of chemistry for a century. Stahl's influence in medicine has probably been equally destructive.

Like many before him, Stahl held to the Platonic idea that the soul creates the body for its own residence and in order to pursue its own interests.

Stahl believed that the soul forms the body and keeps it healthy by something that has been translated as *motions*. If anything inhibited these *motions*, disease developed. The constitutional factors implied in Galen's body humors were downgraded as factors in disease. According to Stahl, all emotions implied a need to acquire some psychologic goal which in some way becomes united with an external object (*introjection*, in today's terminology); the emotion, to be satisfied, might require rejecting or escaping from some external object. The suppression of strong emotions by opposite emotions is very dangerous to health. Medicines act only when taken in favorable emotional states, and hence psychotherapy must precede or accompany their use. A physician must analyze himself, for he who does not understand his own emotions cannot understand those of his patients. Stahl also supposed two opposite propensities in the human body, one constantly and uniformly tending to corruption and decay, the other to life and health. (Bichat accepted this notion as such, and to Freud these propensities became Eros and Thanatos. Neither Bichat nor Freud, nor the many others who adopted similar views, mentioned the resemblance to the Yang and Yin of the Far East, or to the Manichean heresy of the early Church in the Middle East.) Stahl's relations with his students complicated matters. It is difficult to decide which ideas belonged to whom. In some cases Stahl used his introduction to a student's thesis to delineate his own ideas. In later years, Stahl referred to these dissertations (not merely the introductions) as his own works.

Having accepted as established that the Platonic version of the soul-body relation needed no proof, he proceeded to explain all of medicine—*all of it*—on the basis of this superstition.

It would be difficult to appreciate the adulation with which his system of medicine was received, if we had not had a similar occurrence with the advent of Sigmund Freud. Translation of Stahl's collected medical writings into French was prepared and published in four parts from 1859 to 1863, simultaneously in Paris, Montpellier, and Strasbourg (3). Each article in it was followed by ecstatic commentaries by leading medical worshippers. Like any true worshipper, they often had to tell their god what he had actually meant when he was too vague to be comprehended.

The publication of Stahl's collected works signaled a late stage in his influence; almost a century before its final publication, he had acquired a corps of devoted followers in medicine. The enormous growth of psychosomatic medicine in England and, to a lesser extent, on the Continent, was based on published case material showing how the mind not only influenced but controlled the body. However, the English Rationalists and their French followers made the soul an unnecessary concept in psychology and medicine, and the rise of ego psychology in Germany and Austria complicated matters. Von Feuchtersleben, recognizing the solipsistic manner in which each author defined the ego, stated: "That ego of which we speak consists of body and mind" (4, p. 77). To Von Feuchtersleben, the mind and the body acted upon each other, but he added what was to become a century later a cornerstone of American psychosomatic medicine:

For the body would experience nothing of the heavenly contact of the intellect, if the latter were not enabled to make itself known to it through the medium of figurative language, and, if we are to recognize them as applicable to ourselves, all the reciprocal relations of the body to thought, which will further engage our attention in these lectures, can and must lie only in the first traits hitherto developed, of this figurative language. (4, p. 127)

Thus when in the twentieth century American psychosomatic medicine adopted the Stahlian view of the primacy of mental processes in producing somatic diseases—the addition of the idea that the mind spoke to the body in symbols—American psychosomatic medicine had an impregnable, irrefutable system that could explain anything. Nothing could ever be proved, but, on the other hand, nothing could ever be disproved. Difficulties arose when different authors favored symbols that clashed, or when a symbol in some old Yank's thinking could be derived only from one of the lesser Styrian dialects. The main problem was that having the patient believe in the Stahlian theory made no difference in the course of his disease. The situation changed drastically when the physiologic approach to the study of emotion, initiated in Italy by Mosso in the 1880s and by Binet and his co-workers in France a decade later, finally reached America around 1940, and proceeded to develop at a phenomenal rate, in part because of Americans' fascination with measurement gadgets. However, Stahl was at least consistent: he held back both chemistry and clinical medicine for decades.

Thus we see two educated men, almost contemporaries, both

convinced of the Platonic ideas about the relations between soul and body. Yet the ways in which they expressed this belief were opposite to each other, and also opposite to each man's status in the world of scholars. Swedenborg, the mystic theologian, was stimulated to make outstanding physiological discoveries. Stahl, the practicing physician, was stimulated to develop a highly mystical, dogmatic, regressive system.

The men were opposite—and wrong—sides of the same coin.

The late events and ultimate outcomes of the careers of these two men could never have been predicted when first they entered into them. Stahl should have carried out the functions of a healer, and instead he became one of the great dogmatists of medicine. His armchair theories retarded the development of the healing arts during the century and a half that preceded our own era. It was only because some of the oustanding healers of the nineteenth century refused to accept his dogmas that clinical medicine was able to escape complete stultification. The harm done by the recrudescence of his beliefs in America in the mid-twentieth century has largely abated.

On the other hand, Swedenborg, although not a physician, made important contributions to medical knowledge. They were not, however, produced in accordance with his labels, first as engineer and later as philosopher. Moreover, they were only a small part of his massive writings. Most people came to consider him mainly a mystical philosopher, and his careful physiologic and anatomical studies were not recognized, much less appreciated. Fortunately, this neglect of his contributions did not persist for long, because other men, bearing more acceptable labels, soon rediscovered what he had first found. Although nothing was lost except time, it is regrettable that this man's work was evaluated only in terms of the label he bore.

REFERENCES

1. Pratt, F. H. *Swedenborg on the Thebesian blood flow of the heart.* Annals of Medical History 4:434, 1932.
2. Swedenborg, E. *Oeconomia regni animalis.* V. V. G. Williamson, ed. London: W. Newberg, 1847.
3. Stahl, G. E. *Oeuvres medico-philosophiques et pratiques.* Trans. and commentary by T. Blondin. With remarks by L. Boyer and other French

and foreign learned collaborators. 4 volumes. Paris: J. B. Ballière et Fils; Montpellier: Patras; Strasbourg: Treuttel et Wurtz; 1859–1863.

4. Von Feuchtersleben, E. *The principles of medical psychology* (H. E. Lloyd, trans.). London: The Sydenham Society, 1847.

Chapter 11

MISCELLANEA

Homer Bigelow's signature, made according to Henland's method. One can find anything one expects about Homor Bigelow's unconscious mind in these inkblots.

The foregoing chapters have discussed in detail a number of major items in the history of psychiatry which exemplify the role of cultural and social factors in the genesis of psychiatric concepts. There are other items that deserve similar treatment, but because they are of lesser magnitude, they have been gathered into one chapter for brief consideration.

PSYCHIATRIC ORIGIN OF SOME SLANG EXPRESSIONS

Among the patients' delusions reported by authors of antiquity is the feeling of being a ceramic pot or pitcher. This was not mentioned by Hippocrates, Celsus, Pliny, Galen, or Areteus, but Caelius Aurelianus (fifth century A.D.) stated that some patients harbored the delusion. It is probable that he found this idea in the writings of one of the many of his predecessors mentioned in his book. Paulus Aeginata (seventh century) added the feature of a patient's constant fear of being cracked by ungentle handling. This was repeated verbatim, without attribution, by Bartolomeus Anglicus (thirteenth century) and Wier (1583) and also in fragmentary form by Bright (1586) and Willis (1660) and later many others.

The persistence of this peculiar delusion is interesting in itself and also as regards its implications. The French word for "cracked," *écrassé*, became "crazy" in English. The origins of

194

such slang terms as "crackpot" for any person of poor judgment, and of "psychoceramist" for a psychiatrist may be related.

If these slang words do indeed have this ancient origin, they rival "in the groove" or "groovy," derived from the ancient Latin *delire*, (modern English "delirium," meaning not in the groove or furrow).

On the other hand, the word "patsy" has a much shorter history. The word *pazzi* from which it apparently derives is discussed by Father Gregory Martin in 1581. Father Martin wrote *pazzi* as *patzi* and explained it to mean "fooles and mad follies" (1).

The origin of "go climb a tree" is also fairly recent. In medieval Europe there was a widespread belief that witches collected men's penises and hid them in treetops. Hence, to direct an expression of contempt toward some man, his condemner would imply that he had better seek among the treetops for his lost part.

The case of the phrase "rocks in the head" is more ambiguous. A succession of authors described calcifications in various parts of the brain as a cause of mental disease (see Chapter 9). On the other hand, a succession of painters and engravers beginning with Hieronymus Bosch (1485) pictured quacks pretending to remove stones from the heads of the mentally ill.

The word "batty" may also have an ancient origin. The introduction of alcohol into Greece produced an epidemic of mental disease. The victims—Antiope, Lycurgus, and the daughters of Proteus and Minyas—were said to have been made mad by the gods, and after becoming psychotic turned into bats. The word "batty" may be the sole remaining memory of that unhappy occurrence.

INKBLOTS BEFORE RORSCHACH

The inkblot test today is a mainstay of psychiatric diagnosis although many psychologists consider the assumption that it accurately reveals unconscious thought processes to be poorly founded. It is interesting that inkblots and related phenomena were also used in the past in attempts to reveal unconscious elements in thinking.

In the late eighteenth and early nineteenth centuries a number of artists initiated or adopted practices that they believed enhanced the expression of inspiration. These practices included mental free association (developed by the poet Schiller) and the taking of drugs (adopted, for example, by de Quincy). In addition some artists of that era attempted to have chance guide their work. All these purported aids to the expression of inspiration are today also favored by some artists.

Chance-produced blots of various types came to be used as sources of inspiration by artists of past eras. For example, around 1785 the English artist Alexander Cozens (2) wrote a book on how to "assist invention" by the use of chance formations produced by inkblots. His contemporary, Francisco de Goya (3), invented a related process about thirty-five years later. Goya first covered small ivory plates with blackening, and then, after they were dry, let drops of water fall on them. The irregular chance-produced gray and white areas so formed were then embellished with various pigments to become the objects or persons portrayed in these miniatures.

There is no way of estimating the extent to which either of these techniques was used subsequently. Actually this is not a main interest here, since Cozens and Goya intimated that their blots, or the paintings derived from them, were chance-directed and not expressions of unconscious thinking. However, relation to unconscious thinking is clearly suggested in a later book by Cecil Henland.

Around 1900 Henland's book *The Ghosts of My Friends* (4) was published. It is not clear whether this was the original edition of the work or whether it was a reprint of an English edition. In any case other editions were published in England, the last of them in 1934. The book opens with a set of directions: "Sign your name along the fold of the paper with a full pen of ink, and then double the page over without using blotting paper." This produced a symmetrical blot. At present, only four copies of the book are known to exist in America. These are in the New York Public Library, in the Countway Library in Boston, and in the libraries of Brown University and the University of Illinois. However conversations with present and former residents of rural New England indicate that the book was widely known among educated persons in that region several generations ago.

The Henland test differs from the Rorschach test. Whereas the Rorschach uses arbitrarily chosen, stereotyped inkblots, the Henland is based on blots made from the subject's own handwriting. Since the handwriting is itself to a greater or lesser extent an expression of unconscious personality factors, it is evident that the Henland test must be superior to the Rorschach test. Unfortunately, there are no known scholarly discussions of how to interpret the Henland test, although it is possible that some New England attic may some day produce such a work. In any case, the fact that the Henland technique was apparently used merely as a parlor game in rural New England should not derogate the test. It must be remembered that the laughing-gas parties of the sophisticated New England youth of a century ago were the forerunners of today's sodium-amytal interview.

THE SURROGATE MOTHER

The term "surrogate mother" is today a familiar one to all psychologists and to many others as well. Its widespread currency is owing to the prominance given in the lay press to studies on rhesus monkeys performed in an American laboratory during the past two decades. These experiments showed that a warm, soft surface may serve as a mother—at least in some respects—to the monkeys.

This idea is most interesting but far from new, for it was discussed a century ago. The man who gave it prominence was Conway Lloyd Morgan, one of the greatest psychologists of his era. His reputation secured for his books a large number of readers. One of his books, *Animal Sketches* (5), was written in 1891. In it Lloyd Morgan reprinted and discussed material from an earlier book published in 1869 by A. R. Wallace (6). Lloyd Morgan told how Wallace had made "an artificial mamma" for a baby orangutan from a rolled up buffalo skin, and how well the baby had developed. The similarity of this experiment, performed over a century ago, to the modern ones is obvious.

THE DISCOVERY OF THE UNCONSCIOUS MIND

When in 1894 Lloyd Morgan wrote *Life, Mind, and Spirit* (8), he summarized and systematized 200 years of one kind of speculation about the nature of the mind. He had a weakness for triads, as the title of his book shows, and as his statement about the nature of mind also demonstrates. He said it comprised subconscious, conscious, and self-conscious levels. His subdivisions were not everywhere accepted. For example, Prince preferred to divide the phenomena of mind under the headings conscious and subconscious, the latter being divided into unconscious and coconscious (9). (The remarkable propensity of psychologists to think in triads is discussed elsewhere [10].) Although today Morgan's name is known to few physicians, during and for a period after his lifetime he was generally regarded as one of the world's greatest psychologists of the era. His books were required reading for all those interested in mental phenomena. They represented a culmination of nineteenth-century thinking on the subject, and were widely influential in the twentieth century.

It must be borne in mind that however influential his ideas were—and still are—they were far from original. The early nineteenth century was the century of introspective psychology, and all psychologists who wrote during that period discussed with different degrees of thoroughness the phenomenon of unconscious thought, including the idea that childhood events—long forgotten—might determine symptoms later in life. Lecky, in his *History of Rationalism* (7), put the idea in the form of a statement about regression under stress: "The conceptions of childhood will long remain latent in the mind, to reappear in every hour of weakness, when the tension of the reason is relaxed and the power of all associations is extreme." In addition many authors discussed repression of ideas below the threshold of consciousness. This, they said, was particularly likely to occur when the ideas in a person's mind were in conflict. Herbart's many writings, first published in the early 1800s and republished in several editions up into the early 1900s, contained many pages on this subject. Some of these works were still in common use in the early twentieth century.

A curious controversy arose around 1850. The English physiologist Carpenter introduced the term "unconscious cerebration" and, in addition, claimed to have discovered the actual process. His claim evoked ridicule or anger in many philosophers. Bain went so far as to say that all thought was unconscious, only emotion and feeling being conscious. Sechenev opined that conscious thought arose only when some unconscious reflex was inhibited. Holmes stated in 1870 that the conversation of women was proof of unconscious thinking.

It is difficult or perhaps impossible—to find a nineteenth-century psychologist or medical psychologist who did not recognize unconscious cerebration as not only real but of the highest importance. However, although there was a good deal of borrowing between authors, each writer insisted on his own ideas relative to these matters. Accordingly, when in 1894 Lloyd Morgan published his neat, good-sounding, and vague formulation (8), he provided a rapid and useful, but not demonstrably valid, method of explaining any and all psychological phenomena. The clinical observations of Morton Prince (9), published in 1916, were more specifically related to clinical problems. Prince, a brilliant clinician, did not succeed in establishing a school of thought in this or any other subject, which was unfortunate for American medicine.

As all students of dogma know, a struggling new dogma may gain adherents by unscrupulously claiming as its own ideas already known but not definitely attached to any currently recognized personality. Hence, it is to be expected that the disciples of Freud, Jung, and others should claim the discovery of the unconscious. In this connection it is interesting to read Morris's *Six Theories of Mind* (11), a scholarly analytical survey of contemporary psychology, published in 1932. Although the ideas of several dozen leading psychologists of the nineteenth and twentieth centuries on the unconscious mind are discussed, the names of Freud, Jung, or other psychoanalysts are not included.

Although unconscious thinking has long been recognized by primitive or ancient cultures, the idea that this kind of thinking should be considered a part of brain activity did not become accepted until around the middle of the nineteenth century—at least in Europe. Its widespread acceptance in American thinking took another century. It cannot, however, be stated that widespread acceptance of the idea in this country had led to appropriate use of the concept.

COMMENT

The four fragments included in this chapter are all important in a particular way. By comprising small points, they call attention to the fact that not only have the broad and major aspects of psychiatry grown from and contributed simultaneously to cultural and social phenomena but many small and perhaps isolated items of psychiatric history have done likewise.

There is no need to emphasize that what a sick person experiences is just as important in human history as what a healthy person experiences. Since psychiatry involves human thoughts and behavior, it occupies a special position in human cultural and social history.

REFERENCES

1. Martin, G. *Roma sanctis.* G. B. Parks, ed. Rome: Edizione di Storia e Letteratura, 1969.
2. Cozens, A. *A new method of assisting the invention in drawing original compositions of landscape.* London: Dixwell, 1785.
3. Matheron, L. *Goya.* Paris: Schultz et Thuillier, 1858.
4. Henland, C. *The ghosts of my friends.* New York: Frederick A. Stokes, n.d.
5. Morgan, C. L. *Animal sketches.* London: Edward Arnold, 1891.
6. Wallace, A. R. *The Malay Archipelago.* London: Macmillan, 1869.
7. Lecky, W. E. H. *History of the rise and influence of the spirit of rationalism in Europe.* London: Longman, Green, Longman, Roberts, and Green, 1865.
8. Morgan, C. L. *Life, mind, and spirit.* London: Williams and Noyes, 1926.
9. Prince, M. *The unconscious.* New York: Macmillan, 1916, p. x.
10. Altschule, M. D. Only God can make a trio. In *Roots of modern psychiatry.* Rev. ed. New York: Grune and Stratton, 1965.
11. Morris, C. W. *Six theories of mind.* Chicago: University of Chicago Press, 1932.

INDEX

201